RESTORED

AND

FORGIVEN

RESTORED
AND
FORGIVEN

RAY & VI DONOVAN

BRIDGE
LOGOS

Newberry, FL 32669

Bridge-Logos, Inc.
Newberry, FL 32669

Restored and Forgiven: The Power of Restorative Justice
by Vi and Ray Donovan

Printed in the United States of America

Library of Congress Control Number: 2018933866

International Standard Book Number: 978-1-61036-970-1

Cover and interior design by: Kent Jensen | knail.com

Cover image: A kintsugi bowl

Kintsugi is a Japanese process for restoring broken pots with a special lacquer mixed with gold, silver, or platinum. The idea behind the technique is to recognize the history of the object and to visibly incorporate the repair into the new piece instead of disguising it. The process results in a restored pot that is more beautiful than the original.

Bowl photo courtesy Wikimedia Commons, Public Domain

God can restore what is broken and change it into something amazing. All you need is faith.
—Joel 2:25

ENDORSEMENTS

Forgiveness can occur through restorative justice although it is not expected and victims should never be urged to forgive. If forgiveness does happen, as it did in the Donovans' lives, then a deeper healing occurs and all benefit.

—**LISA REA**, PRESIDENT, RESTORATIVE JUSTICE INTERNATIONAL (RJI)
WWW.RESTORATIVEJUSTICEINTERNATIONAL.COM

Ray and Vi have shown a huge amount of courage, first in meeting those who killed Chris, then facing prisoners across the country to challenge them on their behavior and choices, and tackling decision makers about the greater use of restorative justice.

The pedestal that I am putting them on here is not apparent when one meets the down-to-earth couple at first. It doesn't take long to see their dedication, energy, and resolve shine through in the conversation.

—**PAUL SCULLY**, CONSERVATIVE MP FOR SUTTON AND CHEAM

Vi and Ray have managed, though, to create a real force for good from the desolation of Christopher being taken from them. They have channeled whatever emotions they had into spreading the word and showing the world that losses like theirs can be avoided. By their tireless campaigning they are ensuring that Christopher is helping others and changing lives just as I am sure he would have done if his life had not been cut so short.

—**COLIN SUTTON**, FORMER SENIOR INVESTIGATING OFFICER,
METROPOLITAN POLICE

Ray and Vi have to be one of the most generous, inspirational couples ever.

They have dedicated their lives to trying to save others from going through, not only the pain they have suffered, but the pain they openly acknowledge the boys who murdered Chris have suffered.

—**LINDA MADIGAN**

Ray and Vi's story is an ongoing one. Their story will impact and challenge you as you read it. I hope and pray that as you do so, you will receive the love and forgiveness which God offers you today.

—**BILL PARTINGTON**, HEAD OF AFFILIATE DEVELOPMENT, UCB RADIO

The very first victim impact event I experienced with Ray and Vi at Thorn Cross resulted in 53 young offenders making a formal response to the challenge to come forward and to publicly commit and apologize for their actions and commit their lives to Christ. Every one of those young lives has been changed for God and changed for good. Ray and Vi have committed their lives to helping to bring healing to both victims and offenders through their dynamic faith and very powerful incarnation gospel of forgiveness.

Let Ray and Vi change your perceptions and your life as you read through *Restored and Forgiven, The Power of Restorative Justice.*

—**SHAWN VERHEY**, MANAGING CHAPLIN, HMP YOI THORN CROSS

(Please refer to Appendix C to see the full endorsements)

THE CHRIS DONOVAN TRUST

The Chris Donovan Trust is a non-profit charitable organization set up by Vi and Ray Donovan, who in 2001 experienced the tragic loss of their son Chris through unprovoked violence. Using their own devastating experience they want to help to educate people about the impact of crime on the victim, their family, and wider society.

They do so by sharing their story and experience with a wide audience including students, criminal justice professionals, victims of crime, and offenders.

Their story will give you an emotional and real picture of how horrific violent crime is. You will be captivated by the Donovans who talk about respect not being gained through violence but by being true to yourself, thinking about your actions and, ultimately, through forgiveness.

They will take you on a journey with them, from the night they were told their son had been senselessly murdered by three teenagers to ten years later when they met the offenders. Restorative justice finally gave Vi and Ray a voice and enabled them to meet the offenders and ask "why?," a question that the criminal justice system couldn't answer.

Vi and Ray do not sugarcoat their loss or experiences; they open up their hearts. They talk about how crime has a ripple effect and one action can affect so many people. After reading their story you become part of that ripple.

Since the Trust was formed, Ray and Vi have visited over 81 prisons and in some they have been invited to share their story on repeat visits.

As an example of their prison work, during 2014–2017 Ray and Vi have driven to and from Swansea prison, which is a 400-mile round trip, and over that time they have clocked up over 3,000 miles. And that's just one prison.

It's the same with schools and conferences, up and down the country.

Ray and Vi have been recognized for their continual work in promoting restorative justice:

- St Giles SOS Project: Outstanding Achievement Award 2016
- Streets of Growth: Restorative Justice Award 2015
- Winchester Prison Inside or Out: Restorative Justice and Victim Awareness Award 2014
- Sutton Council Community: Making a difference to people's lives by going the Extra Mile Award 2013
- BBC Radio Surrey and Sussex: Local Hero's Outstanding Achievement Award 2012
- Word for Weapons: Dedicated to the cause of Restorative Justice Award 2012
- The Chris Donovan Trust was also The Prison Governors Association Charity of the Year 2015–2016

Ray and Vi are also trained facilitators and motivational speakers. They are also champions for many charities.

In 2018 Ray and Vi were awarded MBEs for their services to Restorative Justice.

—**ROGER FOSTER-SMITH**, CHAIR FOR THE CHRIS DONOVAN TRUST

Christopher Donovan
June 4, 1982–May 26, 2001

DEDICATION

To the memory of our dear son Christopher.

And to our wonderful family for all of your support.

And to all the people along the way who have shown us so much love and support (you all know who you are).

A heartfelt thank you to you all!

—RAY AND VI

CONTENTS

The Chris Donovan Trust   vii
Dedication   x
Foreword   xii
Preface   xvi

1.   Our Story Starts   1
2.   Remembering Chris   22
3.   Bank Holiday Monday   26
4.   In The Coroner's Office   28
5.   The Home Group Meeting   31
6.   The Boys Are Chased   35
7.   The Court Case   40
8.   The Defence Case Starts   55
9.   The Jury Decides   58
10. Vi's Diary   63
11. Meeting Christopher's Killers   66
12. Meeting Jack   75
13. Meeting Stephen   79
14. Meeting Ryan   88
15. Visiting The Grave   91
16. Philip's Journey To Forgiveness   93
17. God Opens New Doors   95
18. What Is Restorative Justice?   107
19. Restorative Justice Touches Our Lives Again   111

Appendix A / Testimonies   118
Appendix B / HMP Grendon   127
Appendix C / What Christians and Leaders Are Saying   132

The Journey of Forgiveness   139

FOREWORD

The first time I heard Ray's voice I was driving through the Ashdown Forest in Sussex, Southern England. It was a sunny autumn morning when the call came through on my Bluetooth headset. "Hello, this is Ray Donovan. I hear we might be able to help you." This was out of the blue and quite unexpected. I had recently learnt of Ray and Vi Donovan from a colleague in the restorative justice community, so I knew who Ray was, and I was lucky not to crash my car in shock at hearing him call me. Ray had called to reach out and offer to do anything we needed to develop restorative justice in mental health. I immediately learnt two things about Ray and Vi, and little did I know how true these things would prove to be. The first was how tireless they are at making links and building community. The second was that Ray and Vi have the most unfathomable generosity. Every time I meet Ray and Vi I am reminded of their preternatural energy and a generosity that they draw from a well that is deeper and richer than anyone I have ever met. Together, they manage to create the impression that there is enough for everyone at this banquet.

Following that fateful early morning telephone call, Ray and Vi came to speak at an event my colleagues and I organized at the University of Sussex, near Brighton, to bring together probation services, police services, the restorative justice community, and mental health professionals for the first time to promote dialogue and engagement between these communities. Ray and Vi came on after a very worthy talk with the ubiquitous PowerPoint slideshow about restorative justice practice standards, but which contained not one example of the lived experience of the pain of brokenness and the power of restorative justice to heal that pain. When Ray and Vi sat down from telling their story, there was a stunned silence and not a dry eye in the house. Their story—what happened to them and their son Christopher, how they found the strength to carry on, and the bravery of how they have turned their pain into hope—defies comprehension and was not like anything we had heard before. That day set the mental health community of England, and perhaps across the globe, off on a new journey. Slowly but surely, victims and the people suffering from mental health difficulties who have harmed them, are being enabled to be in communication with each other to create the possibility that the message of healing and redemption that Ray and Vi personify can be shared with them.

Ray and Vi are two separate people, and the account of their lives in this book makes that clear. But when they are together, you would be forgiven for thinking that they aren't separate at all. They are like the couples at the end of *When Harry Met Sally*, finishing each other's sentences, picking up when the other one runs out of steam, making gentle jokes with the audience about their partner's little foibles. Like musical instruments, each with their own sound, but together making something uniquely interwoven. The lyricism and harmony of their combined voices have been brilliantly captured in the play *The Listening Room*, and here for the first time in their written text. They can make an audience laugh with them and cry with them, despair with them and hope with them. But most of all, they convey a sense of how their anguish, their loss, their togetherness, their understanding, and ultimately their love, make them the most remarkable force for good in the world. How many offenders, or would-be offenders, have gone on to turn their lives around from hearing their testimony? How many lives have been saved, how many parents have kept their sons and daughters, children their mothers and fathers, uncles and aunts, as a result of the way in which Ray and Vi have supported each other to overcome their loss and their private grief?

Ray and Vi will tell you it's not about forgiveness. A curious thing in a book with forgiveness in the title. And yet it is, of course. But the gift that Ray and Vi give the people who are in pain, either because of what they have suffered or because of what they have done, is that there is no right or wrong way to feel or to find a way through. They know that people who have been hurt want answers and the people who have done the hurting often want to give answers. They encourage you to ask your questions, even the most private and personal ones. They will encourage you to give answers, even the most shameful and sickening ones. They will encourage you to own up to anger and even hatred, not because they don't understand that anger and hatred are a poison in any human heart, but because they want you to be accepted for who you are and the truth of what you feel. They understand what it means to be a weak, vulnerable, spiteful, hurting human being. Their life story in *Restored and Forgiven* will leave you in no doubt that they know all about being human. They don't try to pretend to be better than other people. Their gift is something much more profound. In the story of their lives—the awful and tragic death of their son Christopher, brother to Louis, Amanda, and Phil, their own journey to being restored and forgiven, and how their generosity has become the loaves and the fishes that nurture the path to restoration and forgiveness for countless others—they show us all that their faith is a mysterious and unfathomable gift to us all.

—**DR. GERARD DRENNAN, PHD**, HEAD OF PSYCHOLOGY AND
PSYCHOTHERAPY, FORENSIC AND OFFENDER HEALTH AT
SOUTH LONDON AND MAUDSLEY NHS FOUNDATION TRUST

PREFACE

How do you cope when everything around you is turned upside down?

We live in a world today full of hatred and violence, from terrorists to drunken thugs. It seems like everyone is out to hurt someone else.

And when we see these images on our TV, we think they happen only to other people.

We were like that, thinking no one could hurt us. We were a hard-working and God-fearing family. And we trusted God to protect our loved ones.

It is when things go wrong that our faith is tested to the limit.

Do we keep praising God or just give up and turn our backs on Him?

When something bad happens in our life, we have two choices:

1. Trust God
2. Give up on God

We all go through bad times, some worse than others.

We pray this book will be an inspiration and help to you as you go through the inevitable hard times.

At the time of the tragedy you are about to read, our son Christopher was getting ready to turn nineteen. He would have been celebrating his birthday a week after he was killed.

Let me introduce myself and my family to you. My name is Ray Donovan, and I am married to Violet (Vi). We have four children: Louis, Amanda, Christopher, and Philip.

I grew up in a family where violence was second nature. I was also physically, sexually, and mentally abused as a child, so I grew up looking for something, but I didn't know what I was looking for.

I got involved in the occult. I began drinking at a very young age, then I met and married Vi, but inside I was still looking for that something that would fill the gap. I was in and out of jobs; I could never settle down.

I must have had around thirty jobs. I won't be putting them all in this book; I just want to write about the jobs and people I met that I think are important to my life and this story.

If you are like I was back then and are looking to fill the gap in your life, I pray this book will lead you to that point where you realize the only person who can do this is Jesus.

God bless you, and please be encouraged as you read.

—RAY DONOVAN

When the LORD restored the fortunes of Zion, we were like those who dreamed.

Our mouths were filled with laughter, our tongues with songs of joy. Then it was said among the nations, "The LORD has done great things for them."

The LORD has done great things for us, and we are filled with joy.

Restore our fortunes, O LORD, like streams in the Negev.

Those who sow with tears will reap with songs of joy.

Those who go out weeping, carrying seed to sow, will return with songs of joy, carrying sheaves with them.

—Psalm 126:1-6

THE PEACE OF GOD

"I have told you these things, so that in me you may have peace. In this world you will have trouble. But take heart! I have overcome the world." —John 16:33

The date was Monday, July 11, 2011, ten years after our son Chris was murdered. That is a day Vi and I will never forget for as long as we live.

We were getting ready for the most important meeting of our life. The venue was ten minutes away from our house but it felt like a hundred miles as we drove there. We didn't speak a word to each other while we drove. We pulled in and parked the car, then I looked at Vi and asked, "Are we really going to go ahead with this?"

Vi looked back and said, "I'm not sure."

After months of preparation and mediation, in the next twenty minutes we would be sitting and looking into the eyes of one of the men who killed our son.

As we sat in the room waiting for the door to open, I wondered: How did we get here?

CHAPTER 1

OUR STORY STARTS

It was May 25th 2001. I had just started a new job after being headhunted by a large cleaning company. I was in charge of a large area of British Telecom buildings around London, which involved a lot of driving on the motorway. As the head of cleaning I had a lot of staff under me. Things were looking up as the money was better and I would be working only eight hours a day—unlike the other firms where I sometimes worked fourteen hours a day without overtime.

The day was a Friday. It was a hot day and it looked like it was going to be a very hot Bank holiday weekend.

I finished work and came home. It was around 6:30 p.m. and we had the whole weekend planned out. On Saturday Christopher, Phil, and I were going out for the day, and on the way back we would get the weekend shopping, as Vi was working on Saturday and couldn't come with us, then on Sunday we would all go to church and just lounge around for the rest of the day. On the Monday Bank holiday we were going to drive down to the seaside, and Vi would relax on the beach while the boys and I would go sea fishing.

When I got home from work that evening, Christopher was getting ready to go out. Vi was still at work. She was working in a fancy dress shop in Croydon, and Phil had already left for work for his evening shift in a pizza shop in Tolworth. He would work until late in the evening.

I made a cup of tea and was lying on the sofa while Chris was in the living room playing his CDs. That evening he was playing "Fairground" by Simply Red.

Now, Chris would not just put a CD on and let it play. No, he would sit there and listen to every word, and sometimes he would play the same song over and over. He would always say to us, "Don't just hear it. Listen to the words."

There is one song that he liked the most, "This Year's Love" by David Gray. While he was playing his music we were talking and having a laugh together. He was also trying to get me to try on his aftershave and kept asking me what I thought of it. I said it was all right but it was not my thing. He was so full of fun that night, like he didn't have a care in the world.

Then Chris asked if I would drive him to his sister, Amanda's, house to pick up some of his clothes he left behind.

Chris had been living with Amanda for a while because he was working with her husband and they put in long hours; we all thought it would be better for him to stay there as she lived near his job and he would be working until after midnight. But then Amanda and her husband moved, so Chris moved back home with us.

I told Chris I'd had a heavy week at work and didn't think I could drive any more, feeling I might fall asleep at the wheel, so could we do it another day?

He said that it was all right and then put on his white wool turtleneck sweater. I mentioned it was so hot out there and he looked like a fisherman. He then put on his sunglasses and said,

"Do I look cool, Dad?" I answered, "In that sweater you look like you will melt." He gave out a big laugh and said I was silly or words to that effect. We both had a good laugh. Looking back to that evening I think I was the luckiest man in the world being blessed with four great kids.

Chris then said he would meet Richard, a good friend of his, and later meet up with Phil at his job and they would go to a youth leader's house, which they all did most weekends. I said, "OK, have a good time."

As he was leaving, Chris did something he never did before in his life. He came over to where I was lying on the sofa, kissed me on the forehead, and said, "I love you, Dad." Little did I know these would be the last words I'd ever hear him say.

When Vi came home from work, we did what most people do: eat a meal, watch TV, talk about work and how we have the weekend planned, and then go to bed. Well, it was around twenty past midnight when the doorbell rang. I got up moaning, like most fathers do, wondering how two of them can forget or lose a key. Boy, were those boys going to get a mouthful for getting me out of bed.

When I opened the front door, instead of Chris and Phil, there to greet me were two policemen. One of the officers asked, "Are you the father of Christopher and Philip Donovan?"

I answered yes. They then asked if they could please come in. I asked why, trying to think what the boys had been up to. I thought this was because when Chris and Phil were going to school they would travel by train, and not pay their train fare and spend the money on extra lunch.

Trying to think what I could say to these policemen kept going around in my mind. I invited them inside, then they asked me to get Vi out of bed.

They made us both sit down and started to explain that Chris and Phil had been involved in a fight. Chris was badly injured and had been taken to Epsom Hospital, and they needed to take us there immediately.

Well, you can imagine what was going through my mind.

The police had a car outside ready to take us to the hospital, which was just ten miles away, so we quickly got dressed and got into the police car. The officers were driving well over the speed limit with the lights and sirens going when suddenly for no reason the police car stopped. Yes, it just stopped and we sat there in the road. Vi and I started to pray like mad. "Lord, please, in Jesus' name fix this car!"

You can imagine the panic. Here we were racing to the hospital to see our sons and then for no reason the vehicle just cut out and stopped. The officers kept apologizing, saying they didn't know why this was happening. The driver kept turning the key, and then, like nothing had happened, the car started up again and we drove off.

Now, unfortunately, the fastest way to the hospital was to go along the road that was the scene of the crime. As we approached the scene we could see loads of blue flashing lights everywhere. It was like Blackpool Illuminations, our famous light festival. Both sides of the road were blocked off with police ribbons closing the road and cars were being diverted down side streets.

There were police everywhere, which only put more fear into us. What were all these police doing here? It was just a fight. This is a busy four-lane road, with a speed limit of forty miles per hour, but drivers always seem to go faster once they pass the speed camera.

We got to the hospital and standing outside by the emergency entrance were Philip and Richard with a policeman by their side.

Philip told us later that as he saw us getting out of the car he thought everything would be all right now as Mum and Dad are here. They will put everything right and Chris would be okay.

As we made our way into the hospital, a big policeman came up to me and said, "Mr. Donovan, I am sorry to have to tell you this, but Christopher has been rushed to the emergency room and they are operating on him now." He then handed me a watch and said, "Christopher was wearing this," but this was not the same watch I had bought him for his eighteenth birthday. I took it and put it in my pocket. I later found out it belonged to Richard. Somehow Chris borrowed his watch for the night as he always forgot his.

We were taken into a small room with just a frosted window and two chairs. We were left alone there. No one came to offer us comforting cups of tea or coffee; we were just dumped in this room and left with our fears.

I asked Philip what happened. This is his story:

It was around eleven thirty and I was just about to finish work. Chris and Richard came to meet me. I got paid that night and Chris said, "Shall we get a cab to Gill's house?" and I said, "No, it's a lovely summer's evening, let's walk," and we started to walk to her house. [Gill is a friend of the family and the youth leader they were going to visit.] We were walking along and having a good time. Chris took the pizza I bought and ate the whole thing. They met a couple of girls in the pub and had a couple of drinks because that was all they could afford. They got chatting with the girls and later walked them home, and then came to my work so we all could go to Gill's together. As we were walking we were singing a few songs. We were singing "Champagne Supernova" and having a laugh. As we walked along the road, two lads stopped us and said we were singing the wrong words, and we got talking and had a laugh. They told us the right words and went on their way.

If we were looking for a fight, we would have taken on these two lads.

We came to a hill in the road not knowing there was a gang coming up the other side. We came face to face with them and they opened up for us to pass. I went through them first and as I passed one of the boys, he punched me on the nose and broke it. I fell to the ground, then two of them started to kick me in the head and I passed out.

When I came around I saw Chris in the road and the gang running away. Then I saw a car coming over the hill barely miss him and then another car followed and ran over him, dragging him about forty meters down the road.

Then people started to run from their houses and do all they could to help Chris. A woman was holding me and others were trying to get Chris from under the car. As I cried in her arms she kept saying, "I am here." Then out of nowhere the ambulance, police, and firemen arrived.

Chris was in a bad way and I could see by the look on the paramedic's face that Chris was dying. All I could do was cry for my brother and ask God not to let this happen.

Both Vi and I were shocked at this and just couldn't make sense of it all. Why would anyone want to do this? How could anyone leave Chris in the road to die? I looked at Phil and kept saying, "What did you do to start it? You must have done something." He kept saying, "No, all I did was walk through them."

After that we sat in the room in silence and prayed. Then three doctors came in and started to tell us about Christopher's injuries. They said most of his bones were broken. He suffered two heart attacks in the ambulance, and his blood flow to the brain stopped, so there could be a chance Christopher could have severe brain damage—if he survived.

And then they left. I think in our hearts we knew we were going to lose our dear Chris that night but no one would dare say this.

I went out into the hospital corridor and started to pray. "Lord, no matter what happens here tonight, I will always praise You." Why I said this I will never know. It just felt the right thing to say. Just after 3:45 in the morning the doctors came into the room and said they did all they could . . . but Chris had died. It was like something out of a film. This doesn't happen to the likes of us. We are just normal people getting on with our lives. Christopher never hurt anyone in his life. Who would kill him, and why would they want to?

Well, after hearing the news it felt like the doctor put his arm into my chest and pulled my heart out. I fell to my knees crying and screaming and banging my head on the floor. A doctor came running over to me and held me in his arms. Vi ran out of the room because she thought if she ran away she would wake up and Chris would still be alive.

As she ran down the corridor she ran into the arms of a policeman. He just hugged her and he was crying too. He looked at Vi and said, "We will get them." Vi went mad and used a few swear words saying, "Don't make me laugh. You will never get them."

That morning she'd said goodbye to Chris as she left for work and like most teenagers he just grunted back.

The policeman brought Vi back to the room and we were told we would have to identify Chris.

I was trying to look after Phil who just stood there, and I could see in his face he was not taking it in. Chris died on May 26, 2001, at 3:30 in the morning.

After a while the hospital chaplain came into the room. I remember saying to this man as he entered the room, "Do I need you?" We were all crying. He seemed to calm Vi down but I was still sobbing my heart out. I had just lost my dear son. The chaplain looked at me and said, "You need to stop crying. You need to put it aside for a moment."

Why is it that some people think only the mother hurts in times like this, while the father is more or less treated as a bystander?

Well, if ever a person came close to getting a smack in the face that night, it was this chaplain. I yelled at him and ran out of the room to stop myself from hitting him.

I was followed by Gill, who heard the news and came to the hospital to support us. I stood there numb, just looking at her, when she said gently, "I think we should go back. You and Vi need each other right now."

So we went back to the room; I went over to the chaplain and said I was sorry for shouting at him. He said it was all right and asked if we would like him to arrange for us to identify Chris.

(Years later Vi was in Epsom Hospital as a patient and the same chaplain came into the ward and was giving out tracts. He came over to Vi and asked, "Do I know you from somewhere?" Vi answered, "Yes, I am the wife of the husband you showed no compassion to on the night our son was killed." He sat on the edge of the bed and took a deep breath and said, "I have never forgotten that night, and I have learned a lot from what your husband said to me. Now I am more careful when I speak to people who have lost a loved one. Do you think your husband could forgive me?" Vi smiled and said, "It's OK. Ray forgave you for that years ago." The man left the ward smiling.)

We headed to see Chris with the chaplain leading the way. I remember getting in the elevator not knowing if I could bear to see my son dead. I was in fear of what I would see. When we got up to the floor where they laid Chris out for us to identify him, the chaplain led us down a corridor to where Chris was laid to rest. When we got near the room Chris was in, I could not move. I just froze. In the next couple of minutes I would be seeing my son lying there dead. I turned to Vi and said, "I just can't do this. I can't go in there." Then Vi said it was all right and she would go in alone.

But when I saw her strength I decided if she can do it, then so can I.

There were nurses and policemen everywhere on the floor. Outside the room were a policeman and a doctor. Before we went in, I asked if we could donate Chris's organs. The policeman said, "I am sorry to say no, you won't be able to donate."

He then said, "I don't know how to tell you this, but you can't hold or cuddle him." Chris was now to be the property of the coroner. (We later found out that Chris's body was considered a "crime scene." Surely that's not right! A house or a car getting broken into is a crime scene. This is our son. He is a human being, not a piece of property.)

When we entered the recovery room, Christopher was lying on a bed wrapped up like a mummy. They were supposed to make him look presentable for us but they left a tube in his mouth and blood on his face. The right hand side of his handsome face was destroyed—shattered from the kicking.

Then the officer again came up to us and said, "We have to remind you again you can't cuddle or hold him, as they need to do forensic tests on him." I went mad. I said, "Before he left home, the last thing he did was to kiss me on my forehead and tell me he loved me. And if any of you try to stop me from kissing his head, police or no police, you will all need hospital treatment when I am finished with you!"

They all looked at each other and had a quick talk and then said, "OK, Mr. Donovan, you can kiss his forehead but you must not touch him. You must keep your arms behind your back and you must not try to cuddle him." I went over to his body and kissed his cold forehead and in between tears I said, "I love you, Chris."

While all this was going on the chaplain was praying the Twenty-Third Psalm ("The Lord is my Shepherd"). Well, the Bible says we will lay hands on the sick and they will recover, so as I couldn't lay hands on Chris, I pleaded as I laid my hands over him and shouted out, "In the name of Jesus, come back to life." I said this a few times but Vi numbly said, "He's gone, Ray."

It's funny how God works at times when you don't expect Him to. As we were standing over Chris, God reminded me of a time when a man came to our church and preached on Jesus calming the storm.

Jesus was in the stern, sleeping on a cushion. The disciples woke him and said to him, "Teacher, don't you care if we drown?" He got up, rebuked the wind and said to the waves, "Quiet! Be still!" Then the wind died down and it was completely calm.
—Mark 4:38,39

He was saying that this storm was not a natural storm; it was a demonic storm set up by Satan.

But Jesus looked the storm in the eye and rebuked it. The pastor stated Jesus must have said something like this: "Satan, if this is the best you can do, I laugh at you."

And then he said when storms come into our lives, look Satan in the eye and say, "If this is the best you can do, I laugh at you."

I looked at Chris lying there and I said out loud, "Satan, if this is the best you can do, I laugh at you. You took one of my kids; now I am gunning after yours."

Well, after saying that I fell into a policeman's arms and cried my eyes out. He said to me, "Mr. Donovan, we will get whoever did this. No matter how long it takes, we will get them."

He then added, "I hate to have to ask you this, but I have to by law. Is this your son, Christopher Donovan?"

I looked at the officer and saw he had tears in his eyes. I wanted to say no, you got it all wrong, but all I could say was yes, it is Chris. All my life I had no time for the police; they were the enemy. But that man's actions changed my life forever because he was there when I needed someone to comfort me.

Behind the police uniform I saw a caring human who would more than likely have to go home to his wife and family after going through something like this.

We were then taken back downstairs. I didn't want to leave Chris alone in that room; I wanted to be with him. I kept saying, "I am so sorry, I am so sorry I let you down. It's all my fault. If only I drove you to your sister's you would still be alive now."

We went back into the small room, where Philip was sitting with Gill and a policeman. Everyone was coming in to see if we were okay.

We stayed at the hospital for what seemed like hours not wanting to leave Chris all by himself.

Everywhere we went in the hospital we were shadowed by a policeman. We didn't understand why, but later found out that the car driver was there too.

While we were still at the hospital, I had to do what must have been the hardest thing in my life. I had to tell my Louis and Amanda that their brother had been murdered. I called Louis, my eldest son, but his wife answered and said they were in another hospital with their son who was taken ill that night.

After hearing the news Louis, who lived sixty miles away in Chatham, left his son and jumped into a cab and made his way to us.

We tried to call Amanda but her phone kept ringing and her phone was turned off, so the police had to go to her house and tell her the news that Chris had been killed.

After that we just sat outside in the hospital grounds. I remember the sun coming up as the dawn chorus started. Again there were police near us. Even out here we could go nowhere without them being with us.

We then decided to go to Gill's house as she lived near the hospital, so we got in her car and headed off to her house. We were followed by a police car. As we were driving to Gill's, I was sitting in the back of the car comforting Philip and Vi was in the front. Then I said something that got Vi so mad.

I said, "Vi, you know as Christians God will expect us to forgive the people who killed Chris." Well, Vi hit the roof. She went mad and a few more bad words came out of her mouth. "I will never forgive and don't you dare ask me ever again."

Well, the rest of the drive to Gill's was in silence. No one said a word, but in my heart I knew I was right.

When we got to Gill's my phone rang. It was Amanda saying she was on her way down and asking if I could go with her to the hospital to see Chris.

I asked the police if this would be OK and they called the hospital to let them know we wanted to view Chris.

Amanda and her husband arrived and we drove to the hospital.

The chaplain was waiting for us and took us to the room where they still had Chris laid out. I will never forget seeing her tears. It just broke my heart.

We left that hospital two broken people. It was so hard for us to walk out and leave my Chris lying there alone.

We got back to Gill's and a policeman came in and introduced himself to us. I looked at him and asked, "This is murder, isn't it?" And he said, "Yes, we are going down that road."

Our home group leader and his wife came to Gill's to see if they could help, and to pray for us.

It was now around ten in the morning and we both asked if we could go home. We were driven home by Gill, with Amanda and Harris and their daughter, Rena, following in their car. When we got home the place was not ours anymore. It was chaos as it had police, family, and friends coming and going all day.

Another detective introduced himself. All I could say is he had the personality of a snail. He was so matter of fact and I didn't like his attitude. He seemed to have lost all his people skills.

After he left we then got to meet our family liaison officers. They were two policewomen trained to help victims like us and they were the most helpful people you could ever meet.

After a couple of hours another detective was sent by God. We couldn't ask for better. His name is Colin Sutton. He introduced himself and said he was now in charge of our case and would do all he could to bring the people who did this to court. Colin sat us down and told us what the police were doing.

I liked this man from the start because his first words to me were, "Ray, I won't ever lie to you. I will give it to you as it comes."

He then went on to say he had put up road accident signs asking for any witnesses to please come forward.

I got a bit angry and asked, "Why are you calling this an accident when it's murder?"

He said he did this because more people would come forward for this than if he put a murder sign up, and they were also doing door-to-door inquiries.

We would like to give you an insight of what it was like for us. One minute you're talking, the next you're crying your eyes out. Your emotions are running wild. All you want is to wake up from this bad dream and have your loved one back home.

All I kept saying to Vi was, "What am I going to do? What am I going to do? I can't live without him. My son is gone," I just wanted to be alone and cry.

So I went into our bedroom and sobbed my heart out. Louis followed me a few minutes later to comfort me.

The police said they were going to put an appeal out on the six o'clock news asking for people to come forward. They were still saying it was an accident. Then they asked for a photo of

Chris, so they could give it to the media to put on the TV as they made their appeal.

Isn't it funny how people think a cup of tea will make everything go away? We must have had Lord knows how many cups of tea that day.

Every time someone came to the house they would say, "I'll put the kettle on and make everyone a nice cup of tea." Bless them.

Another funny thing is when people are there, you wish they would go, and then when they go you wish they were there. People were in and out all day. And your emotions are all mixed up.

This reading should show how I was feeling that day. It's from Psalm 55:6–8:

Oh, that I had the wings of a dove!
I would fly away and be at rest.
I would flee far away and stay in the desert;
I would hurry to my place of shelter,
Far from the tempest and storm.

I was praying, "Lord, take me away from this. Please let it be a dream."

The police came back later and had made a lot more copies of Christopher's photo and asked if anyone would like one. I thought that was so nice of them.

Vi talked about how Chris and Phil had gone swimming just three days ago and asked her to join them. She remembered walking down the road with them, thinking it was great to see them enjoying each other's company, and how in the swimming pool they were trying to embarrass her by showing off in front of the women.

I remember Rena, our granddaughter, was crying and calling for her uncle Chris and asking, "Why did God kill Chris?" This was heartbreaking for all of us. Chris loved Rena and would spend a lot of time playing computer games with her. She loved the car racing game. Chris always had a red car. How do you explain to an eight-year-old girl that God is a God of love and doesn't kill people, when she has just lost her best friend?

Then it was six o'clock and the news came on the TV. There was Colin Sutton standing by the scene of the murder, calling it an accident, explaining about the fight and the car running over Chris, and asking for any witnesses to come forward. It was hard to sit there and hear how your son died, and then seeing his photo. It just broke our hearts and the whole family started to cry.

Then the police called for the doctor to visit us and all he wanted to do was give us sleeping pills and Prozac, which is a medication for depression, as if by taking this sleeping pill and going to sleep tomorrow everything would be OK and Chris would be back with us.

When the news was over, we prayed that somehow the people who killed Chris would be caught. I remember thinking, "Lord, it will take a miracle, as we are not the royal family and the police won't be bothered with the likes of us."

Time was getting on and the visitors and police started to leave. One of the liaison officers drove Louis home all the way back to Chatham.

Phil wanted to stay at a friend's house for the night. He just couldn't cope with everything going on.

Finally, it was the first time Vi and I were alone. That's when it hit us. We sat there looking at each other trying to take in what had happened.

Vi got up and went into the kitchen. Vi will tell you what happened next.

VI GETS MAD WITH GOD

After everyone had left, I went into the kitchen to make myself a cup of tea. When I started to talk to God I got so mad with Him.

I remembered Ray in the car saying we must forgive. I said, "Don't you dare ask me to forgive, Lord. I will never do that. And where were You when those evil people were killing my son?" I remember I was shouting and swearing at God. I said, "How dare You ask me to forgive! And where is Your protection? You said in Psalm 91:7 that we will not be harmed."

I was hopping mad. Ray was still sitting in the living room when I heard the phone ring and Ray say, "Yes, please come over; we need you."

If I knew then that it was our pastor on the phone, I would have said, "Tell him not to bother coming. I have had it with God and His broken promises."

But around twenty minutes later the doorbell rang. I was still throwing pots and pans around the kitchen. I think Ray knew it would be best to stay back and let me get it out of my system.

Well, our pastor David and his wife walked in and with him came a peace. I said, "Don't you dare give me that Bible stuff. I don't want it, and where was God? Why did He let this happen to us? Go on—answer that one if you can." I was hopping mad.

David replied with something that made me think. He said, "Vi, I love you and I am going to say this in love." Then he said, "Vi, go on. You tell God how you're feeling. Be honest with Him. Shout at Him. Show Him you're angry. You are. God has big shoulders and He can take it. He wants you to be true to Him, so tell Him how mad you are and bang and shout if it helps. But while you're shouting and banging, we will sit here and pray for you and Ray."

After a while I cooled down, and David prayed for me then said, "I don't have all the answers, but all I can show you is love" and he took me in his arms and I cried my eyes out. He added, "When the sympathy cards and flowers stop coming, I will still be here for you both."

While David was praying I remembered the words in the Bible about love from 1 Corinthians 13:4–7:

> *Love is patient, love is kind. It does not envy, it does not boast, it is not proud. It does not dishonor others, it is not self-seeking, it is not easily angered, it keeps no record of wrongs. Love does not delight in evil but rejoices with the truth. It always protects, always trusts, always hopes, always perseveres.*

We sat and talked and as he was about to leave he said, "I take it you both won't be coming to church tomorrow."

Ray told him, "I'm coming. They took my Chris. They're not taking my joy of praising God."

I looked at David and said, "No, I am not going to church. How can I praise God after all this?"

Ray gathered me in his arms and said, "Vi, if you don't go to church tomorrow, you will never go again."

I wanted to hit Ray there and then for what he said. How dare he say I must go to church. Deep down inside I knew I should go but I am very stubborn. You must understand I wanted to go. The spirit was willing but the body was weak.

I wondered if I would ever be able to praise God again and thought this was asking too much of me. He let my son die.

Where was He when I needed Him? Where was He when they were kicking my son to death? And now He wants me to praise Him. That is too much to ask of anyone.

(It was later God answered my question. He said, "Vi, I understand your hurt and pain. I was in the same place as you when they killed My Son.")

I said I would think about it, and David prayed again and they left.

Around eleven o'clock that night, we were both worn out and just lay on the bed. As we were lying there and crying in each other's arms, around eleven thirty the doorbell rang. Ray got up to answer it. I could hear laughing and crying at the same time.

As I was coming out of the bedroom I met Ray coming up the stairs with a big smile on his face and tears running down his cheeks, with the liaison officer Diana following behind.

RAY TAKES UP THE STORY

I went down the stairs and opened the door to see Diana standing there with a big smile on her face. She looked me in the eye and said, "We got them." All I could do was grab hold of her and we danced in the hallway. We both ran upstairs just as Vi was getting out of bed to see what all the commotion was. We all went into the living room and the liaison officer told Vi the news and the three of us hugged and danced.

She told us that two girls who saw Colin on TV came forward, thinking it was a road accident, and tried to put all the blame on the car driver. They gave the names and addresses of the others in the gang as witnesses. The police would be arresting all of them the next day. Again the tears started to flow. Diana stayed for around two hours and she was to become a good friend of the family. Vi and I went back to bed to try to get some sleep. Vi looked at me and said, "I will come to church tomorrow." I was so glad to hear this. After what seemed like hours, in the end we managed to get some kind of sleep.

SUNDAY

We were woken by the phone ringing. It was our pastor, David. He asked if I was still coming to church that morning. I said, "Yes, and so is Vi." After praising God he went on to say he phoned the elders of the church and they came up with a plan.

They would send someone to pick us up and take us to church, but he would make sure we got there ten minutes late so David could tell the congregation what had happened and ask them to let us praise the Lord and to please have some respect and leave us alone. And we could leave any time we felt uneasy. Andrew and his wife volunteered to come to collect us and take us to church.

VI CONTINUES

It was not easy walking into the church and knowing every eye was on you. We were taken to the front of the church where they had seats ready for us with some leaders and friends seated on either side of us.

I thought, "How can I praise God feeling like I do? I have just lost my son." To be honest, I just wanted to turn around and go home.

But then the praise music started and we stood up to sing. I looked at Ray and he grasped my hand and said, "We are going to praise Him no matter what." I don't know how I did it but we both lifted our hands in praise. Somehow it felt right. A peace came over me and I was praising God with all my heart.

I am so glad I went to church because something changed in my spirit.

AS I RAISED MY HANDS TO PRAISE GOD, AN INNER PEACE AND STRENGTH CAME OVER ME THAT NEVER WENT AWAY AND HAS STAYED WITH ME TO THIS DAY.

I am so glad I have a strong man in God like Ray.

When we got home from church later that evening, Ray started to get pains in his chest and the pain got so bad that we thought he was having a heart attack. So Gill and I took him to the hospital.

When we went to the desk to sign in, Gill told the lady what was wrong with Ray and what had happened to Chris. The lady then said to Gill, "These people are not waiting here for three hours. I will put them to the top of the list."

Well, a doctor came and Ray was hooked up to a machine to monitor his heart all within ten minutes. The tests showed that Ray was having an anxiety attack and needed to rest.

CHAPTER 2

REMEMBERING CHRIS

Christopher was born on the 4th June 1982 in Kings College Hospital London. He was a good baby and had blond hair and lovely blue eyes that would melt any woman's heart.

When he was born the nurses put him into my arms before they cut the cord. There was a special bond because of this.

Christopher was like most boys. He went to school and played games with his brothers and sister. While we were living in Stoneleigh, Vi and I were both working in a charity shop just a few yards from our home. Well, Vi had to pop home for something when she heard a noise upstairs. She went to look, and hiding in the wardrobe were Chris and his friend Richard, and Phil was under the bed. The three of them were playing truant from school. Boy, did they get an earful from Vi that day.

Then when Chris was sixteen he flew to the US to visit our son-in-law's brother who lives in Miami. While he was there he got on a Greyhound bus and did a bit of traveling across a few states.

One day he decided to defrost the chicken for tomorrow's meal. Christopher put the chicken in the sink and turned on the tap, then forgot about it and went to the beach.

When he came home the house was flooded. There was water everywhere! The chicken had blocked the plughole.

Then there was the time we went to Greenwich Park for the day. There was Amanda with her daughter, Rena, who was around three, Chris, Phil, Vi, and me. The boys and I wanted to go on the boating lake and have a go at rowing. There were only two boats left, a single and a double, so Phil grabbed the single one and left Chris and me sharing the double one. This was like a canoe where one person sat in the front and one sat behind.

We got in the canoe and were doing OK when Vi called over and said, "Rena wants to say hello," so I told Chris to turn the boat around. He just could not get the hang of it, so I suggested, "Let's change places," and the next thing I knew Chris was standing up in the boat and it overturned. We ended up to our waist in the smelly, dirty pond water. Thank God it was only up to our waist and we could walk out. I looked over to where Amanda and Vi were sitting, and Amanda was on her back laughing her head off and Vi wasn't far behind her. As we walked out of the pond, if felt like the whole of Greenwich was looking at us. I could see Amanda crying with laughter.

But she laughed even louder when I went to the attendant and asked for my money back. Both Chris and I could not see the funny side of it. We were soaked and I had my best pants on.

We went over to where Vi and Amanda were rolling around on the ground and sat down on the grass to let the sun dry us off. There is no worse feeling than water in your shoes.

After an hour or more of Amanda going on and on about it and still laughing, we made our way home. We didn't have a car then so we had to get the bus. Chris and I sat together and the others sat toward the back, as the smell of the pond on us was too much for them, and every now and then Amanda would start to laugh out loud again. The other passengers must have thought she was mad.

Even to this day Amanda still has a laugh about it. I thank God we didn't take a video camera with us that day or Amanda would have sent it to *You've Been Framed!* on TV.

Christopher got a job in a pizza shop with his brother-in-law, Amanda's husband. He started off doing pizza delivery and would use his bike for everything. One Christmas Christopher went to deliver a pizza at a customer's house. There was a party going on and the customer invited him in for a drink. Well, he was there for hours. At the shop, everyone got so worried that they hadn't heard from him in a while that they called the police and local hospitals.

The police saw his bike outside the house of his last delivery and found him. They were not too happy to be called out while he was enjoying himself. Chris just couldn't understand what all the fuss was about.

Another time he saw there was a local record for the most pizzas delivered in one day so he set out to beat it—and he broke the record! He worked nonstop from early morning till the shop closed at midnight, flying around Sutton and the surrounding areas. What he got for his efforts was a golden baseball cap and a Coca-Cola watch that hangs in my office.

Soon after that he was to be promoted to assistant manager, one of the youngest the company ever had.

Then he entered a contest on the local radio and won four nights stay in a posh hotel in Paris for two with £200 (around $250) spending money thrown in.

He gave the prize to us and said, "You both need a good holiday," but he kept the cash for himself. It was a great four-day holiday and we will never forget his unselfish act toward us.

Christopher thought the world of his niece, Rena. He would sit with her for hours playing video games. The one she loved most was racing cars. Rena was about four years old at the time. In the game he would always have a red Ferrari. Christopher loved life and would do anything for anyone.

CHAPTER 3

BANK HOLIDAY MONDAY

MAY 28TH 2001

It was around ten in the morning when I called our pastor and asked if Vi and I could see him along with another church elder, as we wanted to send a card to the driver of the car to let her know we didn't hold her responsible for running over Christopher. At this time we still didn't know if the boys or the car had officially killed Chris.

We went to his house that evening and we all sat down and prayed, then started to draft the right words to put in the card. After a few cups of tea we managed to complete the card. The reason we took so long was that we just wanted to be sure of the right wording so the driver wouldn't get the wrong idea when reading it, as sometimes when you read something it can be interpreted in the wrong way.

When we finally had the right wording, we asked our liaison officer, Diana, to deliver the card to the driver of the car.

When we arrived home, I called Gill and asked if she would print something out on her computer for me. The words I asked her to print were:

Christopher Donovan, born 4th June 1982, murdered 26th May 2001

I also asked her to do this in large lettering, and she said she would.

It must have been around 10 p.m. when she came to the house with the papers she had printed off in a half dozen types of font. I picked the one I liked and put a photo in a frame with the wording above the photo, then asked her to drive me to where Chris had been killed.

When we pulled up to that spot, I got out of the car and I put the photo on a garden fence where some kind people had laid flowers.

I wanted people to know my son's name. I remember getting back into the car and crying my eyes out as we drove home.

Gill stayed for a while and then left. Vi and I were alone again and we both went to bed and tried to get some sleep. We needed to prepare for tomorrow as we were going to meet with the coroner in the morning. To be honest, no matter how hard we tried, I don't think we'd had a good night's sleep since Chris was killed.

CHAPTER 4

IN THE CORONER'S OFFICE

Again our church blessed us, as Dave called to say one of the leaders had a minivan and would drive the family to and from the coroner's office in Epsom Hospital, and he invited all the family to his house for lunch afterward. When we arrived at Epsom Hospital, Colin Sutton and other police officers were waiting for us. He came over to us and said he was told about the card that we had written to the driver of the car and that in all his time as a policeman he had never seen such compassion.

We then all went to the coroner's office. I was consumed with the thought that I was going to see Chris, and that's all I wanted to do. As we entered the office, the coroner, a nice lady, introduced herself and took us into a large room.

She told us that she would be looking after Chris and explained her job to us.

(The coroner's jurisdiction is limited to determining who the deceased was and how, when, and where they came by their death. When the death is suspected to have been either sudden with unknown cause, violent, or unnatural, the coroner decides whether to hold a post-mortem examination and, if necessary, an inquest.)

She started to tell us about Christopher's injuries. It seemed nearly every bone was broken in his body. She talked for what seemed like an hour.

In the end I said, "Please, do we need to hear any more of this?" It was getting too much for me. "I want to see my son." I looked at Vi thinking she was not the same woman I had married. Her face was pale, her eyes red from crying. She looked back at me as if to say, "Ray, tell her to stop, please."

The coroner saw how upset we were getting. She was very caring and loving and said, "I will stop. If anyone has any questions, please see me later."

She then took us to the morgue to see Chris. I remember walking into the room with Vi and Dave, our pastor. Chris looked like he was asleep. He had a smile on his face. They had bandaged the side of his face that was injured from the attack, and around his neck was what looked like a frilly altar boy's collar.

Again, we were not allowed to touch him. There was a policeman in the room to make sure we obeyed the law. We prayed over our son and talked to him, telling him how much we are going to miss him.

THEN IT HIT ME. CHRISTOPHER BEAT ME TO HEAVEN, AND THAT THOUGHT MADE ME SMILE.

When we came out of the room, Amanda and Harris went in. As we were sitting on uncomfortable wooden chairs in the hallway, the coroner came over to us and said, "Mr. Donovan, I have bad news to tell you." I looked up at her and asked, "What could be worse than seeing Chris in there?"

She replied, "I am sorry to say but we will have to remove Christopher's brain to see if it was the car or the kicking that killed him," and then came the bombshell: we wouldn't be able to bury Chris for sixteen weeks.

I looked at her and said, "You do what you need to do. That is not my son in there. That is just his shell. My son is in heaven. And no one can harm him anymore."

VI

I could not believe what I just heard. Ray was right. Chris was in heaven and no one could hurt him anymore. Hearing Ray say this gave me a peace knowing my son is in heaven. This is the hope we have in Jesus.

Not long after Ray and I had given our lives to Jesus, Chris kept staring at us, till one day I was in the kitchen and he was standing there watching. I asked him what's wrong. He said, "Nothing. It's just since you and Dad became Christians, you both don't swear or raise your voice—and it's nice." So I asked him, "Wouldn't you want this peace?" He said, "No. I have my life to lead, and I want to go clubbing and go out with girls."

I looked at him and said, "God is not a killjoy. He won't stop you having fun but He will show you the right way to go about it."

Then the conversation ended and my heart broke.

RAY COMES BACK

After we left the coroner's office, little did we know that would be the last time we would ever see Chris again.

Returning from the hospital, we all went to the spot where Chris had been killed to lay flowers under his photo. Everyone was there: the police, Dave, Amanda, Louis, her husband's friends. The only person who was missing was Phil. He just couldn't handle it all, so he stayed home with a friend.

CHAPTER 5

THE HOME GROUP MEETING

We went home to pick up Phil and took him with us to Dave's house for lunch. While we were there, our home group leader, Andrew, called and asked if both Vi and I were coming to the home group meeting. I asked Vi if she wanted to go, and to my surprise she said yes.

When I told him we were coming, he asked, "Why not come early and have dinner with us before the others in the group arrive?" We both thanked him and said that would be nice.

It was around five in the evening when Andrew came to pick us up to take us to his house. I was sitting in his living room when everything caught up with me—what the coroner told us about how Chris was killed and how we would have to wait sixteen weeks to bury him.

As I sat there I started to get mad and, believe me, I was thinking of leaving Andrew's house and going to my old haunts to get a few old friends together and go after the boys and their families and petrol bomb their homes.

Then Andrew, his wife, and Vi came into the room. After one look Andrew asked me, "Are you OK?" I said, "No. To be honest, the old Ray has come back and I want to get these cowards who left my son in the gutter to die."

You see, the old south London Donovan boy was coming back and I wanted an eye for an eye. I was so angry I wanted revenge. (It is not a sin to be angry; it's what you do with the anger that makes it a sin.)

Andrew sat near me and said, "Ray, may I pray for you, please?" I said, "Yes, please," and Andrew called everyone around me and he prayed for God's peace over me. As he was praying God opened heaven's door and I heard Christopher say, "Hello, Jesus." Well, God's peace came over me. Andrew saw my face and asked, "What has happened to your face? It's glowing."

When I told him what happened while everyone was praying, he started praising God, saying this is supernatural. Well, about five minutes later the Holy Spirit fell upon me and I got drunk in God's Spirit. I was out of control with laughter. Andrew went to his phone and started to call all the church leaders. "Listen to this—it's supernatural," he was shouting.

I was laughing in the Spirit for an hour and forty minutes, and as you know, when one person laughs in the Spirit, everyone has to join in and before you know it the whole house was full of the joy of the Lord.

VI

It was a mad house. One minute Ray was wanting revenge and the next his face changed in front of us all. The anger disappeared in a flash.

And when he started to laugh with the joy of the Lord, all we could do was join in. He was laughing so much that no one could eat the meal that was set out before us.

Ray kept saying in between laughing, "The others will be coming to the meeting with long faces thinking, what shall we say?" This image only made us laugh all the more.

RAY COMES BACK

As people started to arrive for the home group meeting, not knowing what to say or do, they saw the joy of the Lord and started to praise the Lord.

Later I remembered the story in the Bible where David mourned as his son was dying, but when his son died he got dressed and praised God.

David noticed that his attendants were whispering among themselves, and he realized the child was dead. "Is the child dead?" he asked.

"Yes," they replied, "he is dead."

Then David got up from the ground. After he had washed, put on lotions and changed his clothes, he went into the house of the Lord and worshiped. Then he went to his own house, and at his request they served him food, and he ate.

His attendants asked him, "Why are you acting this way? While the child was alive, you fasted and wept, but now that the child is dead, you get up and eat!"

He answered, "While the child was still alive, I fasted and wept. I thought, 'Who knows? The Lord may be gracious to me and let the child live.' But now that he is dead, why should I go on fasting? Can I bring him back again? I will go to him, but he will not return to me." —2 Samuel 12:19–23

The meeting that night was awesome and the worship and prayer was like never before because the joy of the Lord fell upon everyone. We left that meeting not the same people as we entered. The power of the Holy Spirit's peace was all around us.

And after that night this word kept coming to us:

Then Nehemiah the governor, Ezra the priest and teacher of the Law, and the Levites who were instructing the people said to them all, "This day is holy to the Lord your God. Do not mourn or weep." For all the people had been weeping as they listened to the words of the Law.

Nehemiah said, "Go and enjoy choice food and sweet drinks, and send some to those who have nothing prepared. This day is holy to our Lord. Do not grieve, for the joy of the Lord is your strength."

The Levites calmed all the people, saying, "Be still, for this is a holy day. Do not grieve."

Then all the people went away to eat and drink, to send portions of food and to celebrate with great joy, because they now understood the words that had been made known to them.

—Nehemiah 8:9–12

CHAPTER 6

THE BOYS ARE CHASED

We sat up till dawn talking, praying, and crying over and over, not able to sleep—and not wanting to. That morning the police came to see us and told us they had three boys and were charging them with murder for leaving Chris by the side of the road. One of the girls who was with the boys went to help Chris by trying to take him off the road, but the older of the boys said, "Leave him there." They walked off and left him lying on a busy road unconscious, not bothered that a car could come over the hill and run him over. It was this action that made it murder, and they would appear in court the next day.

Every time the TV or radio put something out about Christopher's murder, our liaison officers would have to inform the whole family beforehand, so we had to leave phone numbers where we would be because they couldn't show photos of a murder victim without warning the family first.

Out of the fourteen boys and girls, only four were arrested—one for ABH (Actual Bodily Harm) and the other three for murder. They were charged and taken to court. The one who was charged with ABH pleaded guilty and was fined £200 (about $250) and ordered to pay Philip £100 (about $125) compensation for breaking his glasses.

The other three pleaded not guilty to murder and were put in prison on remand, but somehow they were released a few days later. It seemed the three of them were in a youth offenders' institute and started a fight with some south London boys and got beaten up badly. Somehow their solicitor got them released on bail on condition that they must stay out of the area where they lived. As Colin Sutton was telling us this he said, "Don't worry. If they are found guilty and are sent to prison, the time they served while waiting for the case to come up would be taken off their sentence, but because they are now on bail they will have to do the full term."

The date for the hearing was to be in 2002 at the Old Bailey criminal court. They still had to obey the bail conditions: they were not allowed to come anywhere near their homes so they had to live away from home or be put in prison, and they had to sign in at the nearest police station every week while on bail.

The next morning I opened a book the police gave us. It was called a "murder and homicide pack" with information that could help victims of murder, and I started to read it. When I thought I was having a heart attack, that anxiety was all explained in this book. I had to laugh because it also said people don't smile for around six months after a murder. Well, the people who composed this book don't know my God.

It also said sometimes people have to wait weeks while the police do forensic tests and won't be able to hold a funeral service, so it may help to have a memorial service. After reading this I started wondering, how am I going to bury my son? I don't have that kind of money. I prayed, "Lord, help me. Don't let Chris go into a pauper's grave." I kept praying this for days. I never told Vi my feelings and worries about this.

After reading this I said to Vi, "Why don't we have a memorial service?" So we called Gill and asked her if our old church, Stoneleigh Baptist, could let us hold a memorial service there as Stoneleigh was the church where Chris became a Christian. The leaders said yes, so we set a date to hold the memorial service on the 16th June 2001.

It was around this time that we got a letter from the lady whose car ran over Chris.

It read:

Dear Mr. and Mrs. Donovan,

I was deeply touched by your kind words and am inspired by your bravery at this truly awful time. My family and I offer our deepest sympathy to you and your family and pray that you are able to derive comfort from your faith in dealing with Chris passing. He and you will be forever in our thoughts.

Yours in sympathy, (name withheld)

Getting this letter meant so much to us. You must understand this woman was a victim as well as us; she has to live with the knowledge that she ran over Chris because of the action of these boys who left Chris in the road. We pray that God will give her peace and help her to move on.

One morning Dave, our pastor, came over to tell us the church wants to give us a break to get away from everything. They want to send us to the Isle of Wight for a week to get away from the pressure of the press, and they won't take no for an answer. So off we went, Vi, Phil, and I. Amanda and Louis said they wanted to stay at home and the press wouldn't bother them.

Dave drove us to the Isle of Wight where we stayed at Nick's, a friend's house. Little did we know till we got there, but Dave's mother had died and he was there to arrange her funeral. Even though he had all this on his mind, he was like a mother hen over us all week. He couldn't do enough for us. It was Vi's birthday while we were there and he took us to a hotel for a birthday meal. Even though we were being looked after by everyone, there were times we felt like we just wanted to go home. It didn't feel right, us over there and our son dead in a morgue. We didn't say this to Dave, as he did so much for us and we didn't want to seem ungrateful for all the love and help everyone showed us. We stayed a week and came back home. By now the living room was full of sympathy cards, which I placed all around the wall. Vi asked, "When are you going to take them down?" and I said, "After Chris is buried, as each one of these cards is a prayer."

Now it was about four weeks since Chris died. Then one day we were in a supermarket trying to get back to a normal life—if we could ever have a normal life again—when we both felt people were looking at us. It felt like we had a notice on our heads saying "my son was killed." In the supermarket they were playing music and "This Year's Love" (by David Gray) came over the speakers. We both had a panic attack and left our shopping cart in the supermarket and went home. On the way home again it felt like people were staring at us. It seemed to take ages to get home that day.

The next morning I called a help line that was listed in the book the police gave us, and the lady who answered the phone gave her name and said she was the founder of this help line. We got talking and I told her about Chris, and then I said as a Christian I have to forgive. She started to rant and rave and said, "Don't you talk to me about forgiveness. My sister killed herself and I will never forgive her husband."

Well, I started to counsel her and told her she needed to free herself from all the bitterness and anger. She went on to say that when she prays the Lord's Prayer, she stops at the bit that says "forgive us our sins as we forgive those who sin against us." I was looking at Vi and miming "I want to cut my throat" and for the first time since Chris was killed she started to laugh. After a while I said goodbye to this woman, feeling worse than I did before I called her. It was then I told Vi that we need to get away from here and she agreed. So we called a friend who lived in Devon. We had met her on mission in the Isle of Wight two weeks before Chris was killed, and asked if we could stay with her for a few days. She was only too happy to have us stay with her.

CHAPTER 7

THE COURT CASE

FEBRUARY 2002

The court case was set and the boys were to appear at the Old Bailey, which is known as the Central Criminal Court. The court is in the heart of the city of London not far from St. Paul's Cathedral.

As we entered the court, we were in awe of the size of it. We passed through security and then entered the foyer. Our case was to be held in a court downstairs, and outside each court there are sofas to sit on, so we sat outside the courtroom and waited till the case was called.

Sitting right opposite us were the boys and their families, they were talking and laughing as if it were a normal day. It seemed as if the parents didn't care that our son was killed and their sons were in court for his murder.

We were all called into the court. This was not the start of the case, but was just a hearing to sort out a date for the main case.

The boys sat in the dock and we sat in the well of the court by the door. Their families were just an arm's length away from us.

Where we sat we could see the boys and I remember giving them the look that said "I am going to get you." As I was looking at them, one of the boys tried to hide behind the dock.

Then the Holy Spirit spoke to me and said, "Is this the way to behave? Just leave them to me. My justice will overcome all evil." So I sat there and told God I was sorry and if ever I felt like this again would He please help me to take the anger away.

Until the hearing, the boys were not allowed to come into the area where they lived and were on a curfew, so they could not leave the house they were staying in after a certain time.

One of the lawyers got up to talk, and he talked and talked. Then he dropped a bombshell. He asked the judge if the boy he was defending could stay out till one in the morning to celebrate his sixteenth birthday!

I couldn't hold back. I shouted out, "You're having a laugh!" and I was told to keep quiet, not just by Vi but a police officer too. I was angry because Christopher never got to see his nineteenth birthday, which was a week after they killed him, so how dare he ask this? Again it seemed as if they didn't care about what they did to my son.

Thankfully, the judge said no. I think the lawyer was out of order to ask such a thing in a case like this. Did he not think for a minute how we were feeling?

Then the judge set a date for another hearing to begin on the 12th of March 2002.

On the morning of the twelfth, one of the liaison officers came to escort us to the court. We made our way to where the hearing was to be held but were told to wait on the stairs as the courtroom was still in use and the gallery was full. It was then we realized that the boys, their parents, and family were on the next landing, again laughing and joking. Now our daughter Amanda was getting mad at them for showing no respect; she wanted to go up there and sort them out, but by the grace of God she didn't.

We were waiting there for a very long time, I would say about an hour or more, when there was silence from the floor above so we made our way to the gallery.

Then one of the court security officers asked us which case we wanted. When we told him, he said that the hearing took only a few minutes and the case was adjourned to April 2.

Just as we were told this, someone came up to our liaison officer and asked her if she was part of the Donovan trial. She answered yes and then we were told there was a victims' room on the ground floor in the old building and that Colin Sutton and his team were looking for us.

As we entered the old building, we were amazed by the scale of it. It was something like the Sistine Chapel with paintings even on the ceiling. You could feel both the history and the majesty of the place. It was like stepping back in time.

We made our way to the witness protection room where Colin and his team were waiting for us. I don't think Colin was very happy with his liaison officer not knowing about this room and making us stand on a staircase for over an hour.

We all sat down and had a cup of tea and he went on to tell us that the date was set for the main trial, which was April 2.

We then went home and tried to get on with a normal life, but what was a normal life, when all you talk about is the murder and the trial coming up?

The month flew by and then Detective Jack Regan came to see us and told us that the case would now be held on April 3 and he would be escorting us to and from the court from now on.

WEDNESDAY 3ᴿᴰ APRIL 2002 / THE CASE BEGINS

The first day of the trial we were advised not to go as there would be a lot of talking and then swearing in a jury, so in reality the case won't start till the next day. That evening Jack called us at home and said it is not worth coming to the court tomorrow as the judge and the jury will be going to the site where the fight was so they all can get an idea of the area.

THURSDAY 4ᵀᴴ APRIL

We stayed home all day.

FRIDAY 5ᵀᴴ APRIL

We went to the court. When we arrived, we got to the top of the stairs there were a lot of people standing around. One by one, cases were called and people would enter the courtrooms to hear their case.

Then the time came for the boys' lawyers to ask questions. The lawyers are there to defend the boy they are working for, so it is their job to try to get that boy off and not worry about the other two.

Ryan Seymour's lawyer got up and asked a few questions, which Richard was able to answer. He then sat down and up stood Stephen Andrew's lawyer; he asked some questions and again Richard answered, then he sat down and up came Jack Hall's lawyer.

He went on and on asking questions of Richard but Richard was able to hold his own against this man and answered every question with the truth. He was then told he could leave the witness box.

We stopped for a short break and when we came back Philip was called to the witness box. I will let him tell you his story:

When we got to the court it was okay because we were taken to a witness protection room, and I thought I would be there till it was time to give my evidence but that was not to be. I had to go upstairs with the others and sit in this big hall and look at the people who killed my brother. To make it worse they were joking and laughing. I was getting so upset by this till one of the police team came over to me and said, "When this case is over they will be crying, so don't let them get to you."

Mum and Dad, along with Amanda and her husband, went into the court. Both Richard and I were told we had to wait outside. It wasn't long before Richard was called to give his statement. He seemed to be in there for hours and I just sat there praying, "God, give me the strength to be able to face these boys and be able to answer the questions right."

Then Gill came into the building and sat beside me. She prayed for me and said when it was my turn to go into the court she would be sitting next to my mum and dad and would be praying for me.

Then it was my turn to give my side of what happened that night.

I stood in the dock and was handed a Bible and made to swear an oath to tell the truth. Then our lawyer got up and asked me to tell the court what happened that night.

I then went on to tell the court that I finished work around midnight. Chris and Richard were waiting outside for me to end my shift. While they were waiting Chris popped his head in the shop door and asked me if I could get a pizza for them to eat, so I did. I finished work and as we were leaving Chris had an idea and said, "Let's get a mini cab [taxi] to Gill's house and stay there for a couple of hours." I then told the court that I was paid that day so money wasn't a problem in ordering a cab. I thought about it and said, "No, it's a nice evening. Let's walk instead."*

So we were walking along eating our pizza and having a laugh, and Chris was singing an Oasis song. We were walking along minding our own business when two boys who were coming toward us stopped and said to Chris, "You're singing that song all wrong" and they started to sing it the right way. Chris and both of them were having a laugh. You see, Chris could talk to anyone; he was that kind of person.

Anyway, we came to this hill and looking over it I saw a gang of boys and girls coming toward us. As we walked toward them they parted to let us through, and as I was about halfway I felt this sharp pain in my face. I put my hand to my nose and there was blood everywhere. I put my hand back again to my nose and without knowing what I was doing I clicked it back together again, as the person who hit me broke it. The pain from doing that was too much for me to bear so I passed out.

I don't know how long I was on the ground but when I came around I saw Christopher hunched up in the road, then I heard a car hit him and drag him down the road. I got up and ran towards the car and by then the boys were running, and I remember shouting at them, "You killed my brother." When I got to the car Chris was under it and I was trying to get the car off of him. Then a woman from one of the houses came running out and told me not to move the car in case I could kill him. Then she told me she was a nurse and she held me in her arms, and I was crying like a baby.

---

* This was the second time Chris asked for a ride and the second time he was turned down.

Three ambulances came along with the police and firemen. They lifted the car and got Chris out from under it. By this time there were people everywhere. I remember the ambulance man saying, "He is breathing."

And then I was taken to Epsom Hospital where I was checked over and the doctor told me that if they hit my nose the other way I would have been killed. All I wanted then was my mum and dad to be there.

When I was done with my testimony, our lawyer thanked me and then asked me to look at the photos; he asked questions about where the fight started and other things I can't remember. He sat down, then one of the boys' lawyers got up and was very kind to me. He said, "I won't keep you long," and he asked me a few questions and then sat down. The other lawyer did the same. Then Jack Hall's lawyer got up and he didn't stop asking me questions for the rest of the day. He just went on and on, but I didn't have any fear because I knew I was telling the truth and I just answered every question he pushed at me. In the end he said, "No more questions," and I was able to leave the witness box. The judge made a comment to me on how brave I was and he thanked me. I felt good after that and we all went home.

MONDAY 8ᵀᴴ APRIL

I had a phone call Sunday night from Detective Jack Regan saying Philip would have to appear in court again on Monday, as Jack Hall's lawyer needed to ask more questions. So Monday came and we were back in the court. I'll let Phil continue the story:

I was called back into the witness box and Jack Hall's lawyer got up and asked me, "Did you start the fight?" I said no, then he said, "I will put it to you that you were so concussed on that night that you could not tell my client from another."

Well, to be honest, I was mad at this man for doing this to me so I answered back, "I'll put it back to you that on that night if I was so concussed I would not have been in the police station two hours later." He said, "No more questions," and sat down.

I then left the courtroom and waited outside the court. The court stopped for a break and then Mum and Dad along with Gill came out to see me and Dad was mad at the lawyer for putting me through the weekend like he did.

Then I went home with Gill, glad it was all over for me, and I prayed I did okay and I didn't let Chris down.

RAY

I could see the judge and the jury were not too impressed by making Phil come back to the court to answer such silly questions.

After the break we all went back into the court and our lawyer called his first witness. In came this man. He took the Bible and swore an oath to tell the truth.

Our lawyer asked him his name and address and what he did for a living. He said he was a retired engineer, and then the lawyer asked him what he did in his spare time. The man said for the past twenty-four years he was a special policeman (someone who works for the police for free). Then he was asked to tell the court what he saw on the night of the murder. He said he was in bed when he heard this noise in the street.

"There was a lot of shouting going on," he continued. "Now I live on a dual carriageway. There are two lanes both sides with an island in the middle of the road to separate them. The shouting was coming from the other side of the road and it was so bad I got up and looked out of the window to see some boys kicking another boy who was on the ground in the fetus position trying to protect his head from the kicks. Then one of the boys started to stamp on his head, and then they all started to run off. I remember standing there wishing for that boy to get up but he didn't move. Then a car came over the hill and somehow missed him. I was now praying for him to get up but then another car came over the hill and this one ran over him, dragging him about forty feet down the road. I called the police and then ran to see if I could help the lad."

He was then given a photo and asked if he recognized it. He said it was a view of the road from his window. He was then shown a photo of mannequins and asked if that was what he saw on the night. He answered yes, he remembered the clothes the boys were wearing.

The other lawyers questioned him and again Jack Hall's lawyer asked more questions than the others. He just seemed to be clutching at straws.

After what felt like hours with the cross-examination, the man was told that was all and he could leave the court. After the witness gave his testimony, the judge said the court would close till tomorrow, then we were taken upstairs for a cup of tea. It was in the canteen that Colin came over to us and asked, "Do you know we have one of the best judges in the court? I was looking at the jury, and boy, they are on the ball."

Vi looked at him and said, "Well, God answers prayer. Don't you remember us telling you we prayed for a good judge and jury?"

Colin just sat there quiet. I looked at Vi and gave her a smile.

TUESDAY 9ᵀᴴ APRIL

Next day we were back in court and again we had to go into the courtroom first followed by the boys and their families. I think God's prayer line was full that morning, and I think Vi was feeling the same, both praying to God to help us control ourselves and not do something stupid to upset the court.

Every time I felt like hurting one of the boys God would say, "You do something that is not of Me and I will walk away from this case. Vengeance is mine, says the Lord," so I was put in my place. I had to sit there and just trust God and believe His Word.

People ask, "What is faith?"

Well, faith is putting all your trust in someone you can't see or feel but know in all your heart they are there for you.

The courtroom came to order and the judge came in and sat down, then the next witness was called in. He took the stand, gave his name and address and what he did for a living, then he was asked to give his statement. He started off saying he was at a club in Epsom, and when he left he realized he missed the bus and so he thought he would walk home. As he came along the London Road, he saw some boys and girls fighting, then one of the boys, who he later found out was Richard, came running over to him. He couldn't talk; he was trying but no words were coming out of his mouth, he was so catatonic. He handed the man his phone and he heard the police on the other end.

The witness told them that a fight was going on and as he was telling the police the boys ran off leaving one of the boys in the road. Before he could run over and help, a car came over the hill and ran over him and dragged him about forty feet down the road.

He then said as he was running to help he was giving the police all the details of what was going on. He saw Philip running to the car shouting something at the boys as they were running away and he was trying to lift the car off of his brother, then a woman came out and told him not to move the car and to let the police do it in case he did something that would kill him. In what seemed like minutes the emergency services turned up and took control.

Hall's lawyer made a point of order, and the jury was made to leave the room while the judge sorted it out. The next witness was a woman who was asked to tell the court what she saw on the night in question.

She started by saying she was in bed when she heard a lot of shouting and swearing. She looked out of her window and saw a gang of boys and girls coming up the hill and it seemed they were looking for trouble. She continued:

I came away from the window when the shouting got louder and it wasn't like the shouting before, so I went back to the window. I saw one boy lying on the pavement and some boys kicking him and another one in the road and some of the boys stamping on his head.

I then called the police. I looked out of my window again and the gang was running away, then I saw the boy in the road and I looked down the hill and saw the car coming toward him. I prayed for the driver to see him and brake but it didn't happen. The car went over him and took him off down the road. I ran downstairs to see if I could help in any way. By the time I opened my door a boy was trying to move the car and he was shouting something like "you killed my brother" with some strong words added to it.

*I ran over to him just as a neighbor was going over to him
and saying, "Don't move the car. You could kill him." He then
turned to this woman and sobbed on her shoulder and she held
him in her arms till the police and ambulance came to help.*

The judge then called for a break and we all went into the
hall. The man who took Richard's phone came over to us and
kept saying, "I am so sorry."

I said he did all he could at the time. He looked me in the eyes
and said, "I could have done more to save your son," and he again
said sorry with tears in his eyes and walked away.

Both Vi and I were doing our best to hold back the tears,
then I looked over at the boys and they were smoking and joking.
When Vi started to get a bit mad, one of our church leaders took
her by the hand and led her to a sofa. He said, "Let's pray in the
Spirit and ask God to bring His peace on all this."

VI

When that man came over to us to say he was sorry, I thought,
"He didn't do anything to hurt my son." But here are the boys
who killed him, and not one of them is man enough to say sorry
to my face, and when I saw them joking and looking at us and
laughing I got mad. When one of the church leaders came over
to me and took me to the other side of the court to pray, to be
honest I didn't want to go at first, but I knew he was trying to
help me. So I went and then we sat down and prayed, and as we
prayed I felt the Holy Spirit talking to me. He said, "Don't fear.
I am in control. Be at peace." Then I felt as if my burden was
lifted, like the time I gave my life to Jesus—such peace it is hard
to describe it—but all I can say is the boys didn't get to me after
that, and it was then I started to see them in Jesus' eyes. And I
think it was then I started to forgive them.

IIIII   **RAY**   IIIII

We were all called into the court again and another woman was called to testify. She told the court how she heard a noise and looked out of the window and saw a gang of boys and girls fighting. She also went to phone the police and then she went back to the window and saw one of the boys lying in the road. She ran downstairs to help but when she got to the door it was too late. A car drove over him and took him down the road.

Then she said she saw a boy, who she found out later was the boy's brother, running to the car and trying to lift it off his brother. While he was doing this, he was shouting at the gang that was running down the road. She continued:

I ran over to him and said, "I'm a nurse. Don't move the car. You may make it worse and you could kill him."

He turned to me and he put his arms around me and started to cry, and he kept saying, "They killed my brother. They killed my brother."

I made him sit down and I held him till the police, ambulance, and firemen came. They lifted the car off the boy and then took him to hospital. I remember one of the ambulance men looking at Philip and saying, "He is breathing," then Philip was taken in another ambulance to the hospital and the police took statements from everyone who was there.

I remember looking at the driver of the car. She was shaken and crying. She kept saying, "I didn't see him. I didn't see him."

There were some more legal arguments and this went on most of the day, so about 4:30 p.m. the court was sent home.

WEDNESDAY 10TH APRIL

RAY

Vi couldn't come on the Wednesday, as yesterday was too much for her, so I went with Jack Regan. This morning a man was giving his statement. He said he was in bed when he heard a noise outside his house and he got out of bed to make sure no one was doing anything to his car, then what he saw he couldn't believe.

He said he saw some boys beating and kicking a boy lying in the road. He continued, "I turned to my wife and said, 'Call the police. They are going to kill that boy if they carry on.' He then said he saw one of the boys stamping on the boy's head.

The judge then asked, "Could you describe what you mean by stamping?" He answered, "That would be impossible but I can show you what I saw." So the judge asked him to go into the well of the court and show us.

He left the witness stand and came to the center of the court. He went on to show how Chris was lying on the ground and how the boys were kicking him in the chest and head, then he said one of the boys came up and stamped on his head like this, then he lifted up his leg thigh high and brought it down with such power the noise echoed around the court. It made me shiver to think someone could do this to my son. The women on the jury all jumped with the noise. The man went on to say this was done a few times and then he went back into the witness box.

There were a few more witnesses that day but I was outside trying to get over what I heard from the last witness. I just couldn't take any more and went home early.

When I got home I told Vi what the man said about the boys and how he showed them how they stamped on Christopher's head. I don't think I will ever get that sound out of my head. Even now I can see the man in the middle of the court lifting his leg and then hear that noise. No parent should hear that.

Jack then suggested, "Look, why not stay away for a few days?" So we both agreed. Amanda was there every day and said the witnesses were just like the others so we didn't miss anything.

MONDAY 15ᵀᴴ APRIL

We were in the court waiting for our case in the witness protection room when a boy and his mother came in. He just stood there staring at us. I took Colin outside the room and asked if he knew who the boy was.

Colin said, "He is one of the gang but he wants to give evidence against the boys. He wants to tell the truth."

Then the boy and his mother left. Colin came up to us and said the boy asked if he could sit somewhere else as he found it hard to look us in the face after what happened to Chris.

Then we were called to the courtroom, with us going in first and the boys having to pass by us to enter the dock. The justice system is just plain stupid. They take you to a room for protection then you are sitting in a court where the people who killed your son can pass right by you.

CHAPTER 8

THE DEFENCE CASE STARTS

The boy who was in the witness protection room was called to the stand to give his evidence. He started by saying how they all met that evening and how they were able to buy some alcohol, then later into the evening they went to a party that one of the boy's aunts was hosting. But as the party went on, they were all told to leave because they were too rowdy.

The boy continued:

So we left. As we walked along the balcony to the stairs, two of the lads saw a motorbike in the car park below and shouted to the rest of us, "Let's take the bike." But one of us said, "No, let's leave it."' As we made our way down the stairs to the street, the two boys went to look at the bike. We all started to walk up the road. I remember we stopped outside a Chinese take-away and, to be honest, in a way we were making a lot of noise, then we started to walk up the road when the other two came running behind us shouting at each other about the bike, as one of them had a change of mind about taking it.

I remember walking over the hill and there were three lads coming toward us, then the next thing I knew was one of the lads was on the ground with blood all over his face and some of the boys started to kick him. I then saw one of the lads come over to help the one on the ground and the next thing I knew was he was on the road with three of the boys kicking him; I did no more but ran away as I didn't want to get involved in what they were doing. I remember walking along alone. I don't remember how long it was when I left the fight, but the others caught up with me and asked me why I left. I told them I didn't want anything to do with what had happened.

We then went to one of the boys' homes and sat there trying to work out an alibi. We were going to say we were in the house all night but we couldn't say this because his parents were home all night, so we had to think of something else. I remember Jack Hall hiding under the table shaking and biting his nails. Then there was a knock on the door and it was two of the girls. One of them was sick after what she witnessed. The elder girl shouted, "What was that all about? You killed him." Then one of us called his aunt to look down the road to see what was happening. She said she could see police, ambulance and firemen up the road. We just sat there not knowing what to do, then Jack Hall kept going in and out of the room. He lost it big time.

He said that's all he could remember and he left the stand.

Then it was the time for the boys to give their side of the story. It seemed none of them had anything to do with Christopher's murder. In fact one of the boys went home and that morning went fishing with his dad. While we were sitting at home crying at the loss of our son, this boy goes fishing with his dad as if it was just a normal day.

Then the next two boys gave their evidence and it was almost word for word except for the fishing.

Next it was time for their witnesses to come forward. This was to be a farce because the boys were on remand. The rules were they were not allowed to come within so many miles of where they lived and they also had to sign in at a police station every day.

Now, I don't know how they found out, but the police caught Jack Hall in his dad's shop along with two girls who were going to be witnesses for him. All this was caught on video camera but there was no sound, so the police could not prove they were talking about the case, but they still arrested them all the same.

The night before the girls were called to give evidence, I went to Gill's house. We sat and talked about the case. I said to her, "I am fed up with all the lies." She suggested, "Let's pray the truth will come out," so we started to pray. We prayed the truth will come out and the spirit of lies will leave in the name of Jesus.

The next day one of the girls was called to the stand, and every time she was asked a question Hall's lawyer would stand up and call a point of order and the jury was told to leave the court while this was sorted out.

The girl was warned not to say anything about being arrested in the shop and to just talk about the night in question. The jury was called back in then a question was asked and again the jury was sent out. Then after lunch she was still in the stand when she was asked a question, and before you could blink an eye she said, "Are you talking about when we got arrested in Jack's dad's shop?"

The jury sat upright when she said this and the other two lawyers were going at her tooth and nail.

You see, God answers prayer.

The lawyers gave their closing statements and then the judge gave his summing up. This took a few days.

The date is now Thursday May 9th 2002.

CHAPTER 9

THE JURY DECIDES

It was almost a year since Chris was killed and now the fate of the three boys in the dock was down to twelve jurors.

The judge sent the jury out and we all waited in the foyer for the jury to come back with a verdict. But the day went on and on. I remember Jack Regan saying they won't have a verdict today, so he took Vi and a few others for a walk around the city.

I remember sitting and watching Stephen Andrews as he was looking out of a window at the traffic below. I saw them talking but this time they were not laughing. The day went on and late in the afternoon we were called into the court and the jury was called in. The judge asked them if they had come to a verdict. The foreman said no, so the judge sent them home for the day.

FRIDAY 10TH MAY

Still no verdict. The jury was sent home for the weekend.

MONDAY 13TH MAY

The court started and the jury was sent out to deliberate, then by lunchtime we were called in again. The foreman of the jury said they were having trouble coming to a verdict, so the judge sent them back into the jury room saying they could have a majority vote of ten jurors. We all went outside and as we were talking our lawyer came up to me and said, "Mr. Donovan, I have some bad news," and he went on to say that two will go down but one will walk. I looked at him and said, "This morning I asked God what the verdict will be, and He answered that all three are going to jail, so I will believe Him."

No sooner did I answer him than we were called into the court again. The judge entered the court and told the usher to move the boys' parents to the well before he called in the jury, so they had to sit on the other side of us and look us in the eye.

Then the jury was called and the usher asked if they had a verdict. The foreman said yes and the usher called out the boys' names one by one.

He said, "Stephen Andrews. Do you find him guilty or not guilty of murder?" The foreman answered, "Guilty." As he said this, there was screaming from the public gallery, and as the boy was taken down to the cells a young girl called out, "I will wait for you."

Then the usher asked the foreman, "How do you find Ryan Seymour? Guilty or not guilty of murder?" The foreman answered, "Guilty." Ryan started to cry and was holding rosary beads in his hands. He was shaking and he too was taken to the cells. We looked over at his mother and father crying and sobbing.

Then the usher asked the foreman, "Do you find Jack Hall guilty or not guilty?" The foreman answered, "Guilty," then Jack Hall shouted, "I didn't do it, Dad!" (Remember these words.) As they were taking him to the cells, his dad held out his right hand in a closed fist and shouted, "Hang in there, son." He was ordered to be quiet.

The judge set a date for sentencing: 19th June 2002.

When the judge left the court Colin said, "Come upstairs for a cup of tea and let their parents sort themselves out."

Now when the boys were found guilty, no one got up and shouted. Everyone cried. This was not a happy day. As I looked at the parents I said to Vi,

"THERE ARE NO WINNERS. WE ALL LOST A SON TODAY."

It was when I looked at the parents and saw them crying that I started to see them as Jesus saw them and knew then I could forgive the boys.

We went to the canteen upstairs and the police were on the landing outside phoning their police stations with the verdict.

I was sitting at the table with Philip and our church leader and Detective Jack Regan. We were sitting there not saying a word when the door of the canteen opened, and looking up I saw one of the fathers just standing there. His eyes were red from crying and he looked at me, held open his arms and said, "Sorry." I got up, went over to him and I don't know where I got the strength from, but I held this man in my arms and hugged him. I said, "We have been praying for you and the other families, and no one is coming after you or your family."

After a while we parted and he went to get his tea and then left. When Vi and Amanda came back and heard what happened, they couldn't believe it. This is not Ray. He wouldn't do something like that. Well, with God all things are possible. Amen.

WEDNESDAY 19TH JUNE

It has now been five weeks and two days since the boys have been found guilty and we were again back in the Old Bailey to hear how many years they are going to get.

We all waited in the canteen for the case to be called. The same father came into the canteen and this time he had to pass our table to get to the counter to buy a cup of tea. As he passed I noticed this man was carrying his son's guilt, so when he was returning with two cups of tea in his hands and came toward our table, I got up and held out my hand. He put his cups down and took my hand.

I said, "We have not come today to gloat over your son. I just want to see the ending to all this." He answered, "If I was in your shoes, I would feel the same too."

He then went on to talk about what happened a few weeks before. He said, "I followed you and saw you sitting at the table and said to myself, 'OK, let's get it over here and now.'" He was expecting me to hit him, but when I got up and put my arms around him he couldn't believe it.

I told him that it wasn't me; it was all Jesus. He went on to say he was not religious. I answered, "Nor am I; I am a Christian." We talked for about ten minutes or more then he went to give his wife her tea.

We both walked down the stairs toward the court together.

The police said they have never seen anything like that in all their time in service, two dads talking like we did. I pray they, along with the father, always will remember that day and one day they will all find Jesus.

You could say both of us had a restorative justice meeting that day. Maybe this was the first ever meeting like this for murder.

We were called into the court, and before the judge gave out the sentences he described the attack as "gratuitous drug- and alcohol-provoked mob violence."

Stephen Andrews and Ryan Seymour were given life sentences and Jack Hall was ordered to be detained during Her Majesty's Pleasure, which is like a life sentence for young people.

Ryan Seymour was sentenced to be detained for nine years, Stephen Andrews for ten years and Jack Hall for six years, and then the judge sent them down.

[In the UK a judge determines the length of time that a prisoner will spend of his life sentence in prison. This varies greatly and can be from a few years to the prisoners whole life. Once the prisoner has served their sentence in prison, they then spend the rest of their life on parole in the community instead of being in prison. If they commit another crime they will be recalled and sent back to prison.]

A week later we were in church and Vi went to talk to a friend. She was upset by the short sentences and the friend asked her, "Vi, how long is enough?"

VI

Yes, how long is enough? Even if they were put in prison for a hundred years, it still wouldn't bring Chris back to us. So I had to trust God in all this and pray for His peace.

CHAPTER 10

VI'S DIARY

The diary starts off with a prayer from Vi:

> *Dear Father, we are five weeks into the trial of Andrews, Seymour, and Hall, who are the people accused of the murder of Christopher. There have been some hard times in the last five weeks and I have at times not known what to think about it all. But You have given me the grace to follow through and to hold fast. Father, I thank You for it. You have given us a good jury, very thorough in their work, a good judge, and most of all a good barrister (QC).*
>
> *Thank you, Lord.*

THURSDAY 9ᵀᴴ MAY 2002

Jury sent out.

FRIDAY 10ᵀᴴ MAY 2002

The jury is still out deliberating their verdict. We have to wait until Monday. We hope for a verdict then.

Our friends Tom and Isabel came around tonight with their children, and later in the evening the children gave their lives to the Lord. Oh what *joy*. God has lifted my spirit tonight Thank you, Jesus, for their salvation.

Also Tom and Isabel gave us a card and in it was a reading from Psalm 126:3–6:

The LORD has done great things for us, and we are filled with joy.

Restore our fortunes, LORD, like streams in the Negev.

Those who sow with tears will reap with songs of joy.

Those who go out weeping, carrying seed to sow, will return with songs of joy, carrying sheaves with them.

—Psalm 126:3–6

Pauline gave that to us in June 2001.

I guess the Lord wants us to know that it's still there.

Thank you, Lord, for reminding us.

I am trying not to be afraid of the waiting for the verdict. I want justice for Chris, but I also want to be able to forgive once and for all.

Lord, help us to move on. Amen.

MONDAY 13ᵀᴴ MAY 2002

Well, we have the verdict and all three of the boys have been found guilty of murder.

They will be sentenced in about four weeks.

One of the boys' fathers, Mr. Seymour, came upstairs and looked at Ray and said, "I'm so sorry."

Ray responded by hugging him and telling him he forgives him and the others.

(Hallelujah)

Ray always said he wanted someone to say sorry. God answered his prayer.

It's been a long year, a learning time. Now we can close the chapter on this terrible time.

I felt a terrible sadness come over me in the court when the verdicts came.

All three defendants were crying and their parents were terribly sad.

Four lives have been lost for nothing.

WEDNESDAY 19ᵀᴴ JUNE 2002

The sentencing is done.

Andrews got ten years.

Seymour got nine years.

And Hall got six years.

It was very quiet in the courtroom. Jack Hall prayed with rosary beads.

I pray that these boys will come to terms with acknowledging their crimes and even make peace with God and come to know Jesus as their Savior.

As for myself, Ray, Louis, Amanda, and Philip, we have been left to pick up the pieces after all this and get on with our lives. It isn't proving easy.

In fact it feels harder now than ever, but somehow we will go on for Christopher's sake.

MEETING CHRISTOPHER'S KILLERS

From the night Chris was killed up to the end of the court case, we had police, liaison officers, and other people around us, but after the court case these people all went their own way.

And for the first time in a year we were alone.

There were no police to come around with more news or to pick us up to go to court.

It was over for them; their job was done and they had other cases to sort out.

But for me and my family, we had to try to get back to some kind of normal life—if that was at all possible. But with Jesus beside us I knew things would be all right and we would be able to move on.

Not long after the court case, we got a call from a national TV program called *Trisha*. This was a talk show. We were invited to come on and talk about how we forgave Christopher's killers.

The show was shown on TV about three months later. I was at home when my phone rang. It was a local church. They informed me that the wife of Stephen Andrews had just called and said Stephen saw us on the *Trisha* show and would like to meet us, as he is having nightmares. I was stunned and asked for their number and said I will call back after I phone Vi at work.

I called Vi and relayed the message. The phone went quiet for a minute, then with words that are not Christian, Vi said, "He should have our ******* nightmares!!"

I said, "Hold on, Vi. When we left the court that day, we left with nothing but lies in our ears, and now we have a chance to hear the truth."

Vi calmed down and said, "OK. Arrange a meeting."

So I called the church back and got his wife's phone number.

On the phone she said she had been trying to find us for a while. She even stood by the cemetery gates hoping she would see us drive in.

I arranged for us to meet her in a public place, so I picked a fish restaurant. We took a friend with us so she couldn't later say we were rude to her or something to that effect.

We arrived first and about ten minutes later she arrived. We ordered a meal (again, this might have been the first restorative justice meeting like this in the UK).

After the small talk we got down to what the meeting was about. The first thing I said was that I didn't know he was married. She looked at us and answered, "When Stephen was on bail [remember, his bail conditions were he couldn't enter the Kingston area and had to move away from home], we met, fell in love, and got engaged, and we got married in Feltham Prison."

Vi and I looked at each other. Here is this man wanting

to meet us because he is having nightmares and showing no remorse. While we're mourning and burying Christopher, he is getting on with his life as if nothing happened.

The meeting lasted around two hours and in the end both Vi and I agreed to meet Stephen.

Then I made a big mistake. I called the probation services.

Back then, no one was trained in restorative justice, so no one had a clue how to handle this—victims wanting to meet their son's killer.

The phone rang a couple of times and a lady answered. I told her about our meeting and how we would like to meet Stephen. She went quiet and then had lots of questions, like, "Why on earth would you want to meet him?" Vi always says maybe the woman thought we wanted to meet up with him to harm him.

She was on the phone for a long time speaking to the two of us and then made an appointment to come and see us.

About a week later the doorbell rang and Vi answered it. There were two of them at the door and Vi invited them in. I got up to shake their hands. After a quick hello I sat back down again. As Vi invited them to take a seat, one walked over to where I was sitting and in a very loud voice she pointed her finger at me and said, "Ray, go upstairs while we speak to Vi."

They asked Vi so many questions and wanted to know why and what was the purpose of us wanting to meet Stephen.

Then after what felt like hours she ended saying, "Go upstairs and tell Ray to come down."

It was the same for me, question after question, and then the meeting ended with her saying she will visit him in prison and get back to us.

Not long after they left, I was just numb and Vi started to cry.

These people are used to dealing with offenders and forget how to speak to victims.

Not long after meeting Stephen, she came back to us and said she was happy for the meeting to go ahead but she still needed to visit him a few more times before we could meet him.

Then after a couple of months this woman called to say that Stephen wants to cancel the meeting as he thinks he's not ready and can't meet with us. After a pause I said, "I'm not surprised, because if you treated him the same way you treated us, it's no wonder he backed out." And I hung up the phone.

Not long after the *Trisha* show, we got a phone call from a producer from the BBC asking us if we would be interested in taking part in a documentary for their Everyman program. The title was "*The Sun* Says Sorry."

The program was about the Hillsborough football disaster in 1998 when ninety-six Liverpool supporters were crushed to death in a stampede. This was the worst sports tragedy in UK history.

The Sun newspaper reported bad things about the way the fans acted, saying things like fans were robbing the dead and so on. Because of this reporting, newspaper shops in Liverpool will not sell *The Sun* newspaper to this day.

The producer went on to question us about how we forgave and had us on the phone for a long time firing questions at us, and when he was done he made an appointment to meet us.

The program was about five stories of how some people forgive and others won't let go.

We had the producer and the camera and sound man almost living with us for around four months.

They took over our house, taking photos and shelves off the wall. His reason for this was that viewers will be looking behind us thinking, "I wonder where they got that from," etc.

Our poor parakeet had to go in the back garden.

They even filmed Vi hanging our laundry up in the back garden about twenty times.

He asked if they could film me at Christopher's grave, which we agreed to. He went off to get permission from the Council to film at the cemetery, so we were able to get the shots he wanted.

Then one day he came to our house and dropped a bombshell. He said he visited all three offenders in prison, and only one is very remorseful. We wanted to know who it was, and he said it was Ryan.

He then had a great idea. "Why not compose a letter, and I will give it to him?"

So I went up to my office and wrote this letter to Ryan:

Dear Mr. Seymour,

I am sending you this letter to let you know that both my wife and I have been praying for you.

We want you to know that we forgive you for what you have done.

This doesn't mean you are let off the hook. There must be justice for what you and the others have done, as we are sure you understand.

And we pray that one day we could meet you in prison and show you that our forgiveness is not all talk. We would like to tell you face to face how much you are forgiven.

We both feel you have been tormented thinking about that tragic night. This is not very good for your health, going over the past and thinking "what if" and "if only."

Thinking of the past this way can only keep you in that place, so it's time to move on. What's done is done. There is nothing anyone can do to change it.

We pray God will bless you and your family.

A couple of weeks later the producer returned with a letter from Ryan, which he asked us to read on camera, while filming in London, so Vi read the letter to camera:

Dear Mr. and Mrs. Donovan,

I am sending you this letter to say thank you for taking the time to write to me.

I am very happy to accept your forgiveness although at times I find it hard to forgive myself and the others who played a part in what happened that tragic night.

I hope that we will meet one day as there is a lot I want to say to you. I don't think that it is the same doing it in a letter as it would be face to face. I also have a lot of feelings around what happened that night and I cannot express them in a letter.

I hope to meet you one day.

Yours sincerely,

Ryan Seymour

The producer asked what if he could arrange for us to meet Ryan? Would we be up for it? We both agreed, and off he went to Aylesbury Prison to meet with the prison governor so they could work out how to do this.

But the governor, thinking he knew best, said yes, he would be happy to film this—on one condition. If every member of Ray's family says yes, it will go ahead; but they didn't.

After that program, we sent all three a letter saying we forgive them and we won't bother them again, and if ever they want to meet us the ball is now in their court.

Then in 2011 we held a ten-year memorial service for Chris. We don't have memorial services but we felt we needed to do something to celebrate the lives that have been changed because of his story.

The memorial was a time of celebration. We started with a prayer, then we played "Slipped Away" by Avril Lavigne, with PowerPoint photos on the screen of Chris from the day he was born to a month before he died.

Everyone had a tear in their eyes. Then after the song I got up and said, "OK, we had our cry now. If Chris was here, this is what he would say: 'Let's party!'"

We called up a Christian group to sing. The memorial was on for three hours, and one man came up to me and said, "I never thought I would be standing up dancing and clapping my hands not only in a church but at a memorial service."

Chris would have loved to have heard this.

We invited a few charities to come along and put up tables and promote their work.

After the service Sian West, the CEO from one of the charities, came over and said she would love to help our charity. We both looked at her and said we couldn't afford her. She then said she would do it for free. (She is still with us to this day.) Then she asked, "How come you have been doing prison work for so long and you haven't met the people who killed Chris?" So we told her about what happened and how we told the boys we wouldn't bother them again, and it's up to them to contact us if they want to meet.

Sian asked if her charity could try setting up a meeting. Vi and I had a talk about it and said, "OK, let's give it another try."

About three weeks later the phone rang. It was Sian to say they had contacted a charity that facilitates restorative justice meetings and they were very happy to take up our case.

The charity phoned us and arranged a meeting a week later. These two people came into our living room and sat down. After shaking hands the first thing they said was, "What are your needs? What can we do for you?"

In the years after Chris was killed, no one had ever asked us that.

The only one of Christopher's killers we were going to meet was Ryan, as we were told he was the most remorseful of all three.

The interview lasted over an hour and they asked us what questions we would like to ask him.

We wanted to know what courses he had been doing while in prison. What we wanted to know was, is he trying to do something with his life or is he just laying around?

We said, "Please tell him he is forgiven." The meeting ended and they both left.

Then around two weeks later they returned. We couldn't believe what they had to tell us. They said they had visited all three, and all three would like to meet us!

We just didn't know what to say, because we thought the other two didn't care and were just doing time without giving us a thought.

We both thought about it and said yes.

Then I said, "We won't meet them in prison," as their release dates were not too far away, which would make it easier for them to meet us, and we didn't want people thinking they met us only to get time off their sentence.

(When an inmate agrees to meet their victim through Restorative Justice, they don't get any time taken from their sentence for doing this.)

So off they went to arrange a meeting and find out who will be coming out of prison first.

After a couple of months they came back and informed us that Jack will be out first.

Then they had other questions, like who would you like to be in the room first?

I thought about it and said me. They asked why. I answered, "When he comes through the door I would like to shake his hand." They looked at me as if I was mad.

They went all the way to the prison he was kept in and told him what I said, and returned to us about a month later and said, "What if he doesn't want to shake your hand?" I answered, "It's there for him to shake. He can take it or leave it."

After a few more months of them working out the risk assessments, they were happy for the meeting to go ahead.

CHAPTER 12

MEETING JACK

Jack was released from prison, and the meeting would go ahead three weeks after his release. It would take place in a communal hall just down the road from where we lived. They gave us a timetable, which read something like this:

You both will arrive at 12:15 and sign in.

We will come down and take you to the room at 12:20.

Jack will arrive at 12:35 and will come into the room at 12:45.

This is done so no one meets in the car park as things could be very awkward for both parties.

Vi and I drove to the meeting not saying a word to each other until then we pulled into the car park. Even after months of mediation we still had a bit of doubt as to meeting him. Were we both still willing?

Then it was like we were in unity. We looked at each other and both said together, "Yes."

When we entered the room, the first thing we saw were seven chairs set out in a circle. The reason there were seven was because you can bring a support person with you. We asked Sian if she would like to support us. She said it would be an honor.

At the meeting place, there is the main room and what they call a "time-out" room. This is only used if something is said that the offender or victim may not like to hear. They can call for a time-out and go to the room with their supporter and one of the facilitators.

There were also sandwiches and tea and coffee on a table.

Each chair had a name on it and we were asked if we were happy with the arrangement. We both answered yes.

We sat down and waited for Jack to arrive. One of the facilitators went downstairs to escort him to the room. From that moment, all I did was stare at the door and wait for it to open.

Then after what seemed like eternity, the door handle turned and in walked the facilitator followed by Jack and his probation officer. The first thing I noticed was he was wearing a suit with a shirt and tie and polished shoes.

Now that is respect.

As he entered the room, I got up out of my chair and opened my arms, and he walked into them and whispered, "Thank you." I must admit I don't know how I did this. We both shed a tear and he walked over to Vi and asked, "May I hug you?"

Vi held out her arms and answered, "Yes. And by the way, we both forgive you."

More tears, and for several minutes none of us could sit down, then the facilitators asked us to begin.

So we all sat in our chairs, and Jack started to tell us the events that led to Christopher's murder that night. He asked if we would keep it confidential, which we agreed to, but we can tell you this much.

The first thing he said was it wasn't Philip's fault. "It was all us. We were out trying to prove ourselves that night and we ended up killing Chris," then he went on to let us know what he did when he came out of prison. He told us he went to the spot where Chris was killed and laid flowers in his memory. To be honest, I thought the first thing he would do was to go to the pub and have a pint of beer to celebrate his freedom, but this wasn't the case.

He then went on to say that he has been following our prison work and that Chris would be very proud of us.

He is now on parole for the rest of his life and if he does anything wrong, he will be recalled and sent back to prison. He also will never be allowed in the US, Canada, Australia, New Zealand, and some other countries around the world.

He went on to talk about what it is like to be on parole. He told us he was in a pub having a beer when a fight broke out at the other end of the bar, and he had to leave his beer and run out of the bar. Just by being there he could have been arrested and recalled back to prison.

Now remember, in court when he was found guilty, he shouted to his father, "Dad, I'm innocent. I didn't do anything!"

Well, this same young man looked at us and said, "While I was in prison, I fought the system and then I was put in a victim awareness course, something like what you do in prisons."

(The course was the Sycamore Tree and it is exactly what we do in prison.)

He went on to say, "They invited a victim to come and tell their story, and it was a little old lady who had her home broken into, and from that day to this I can't get Chris out of my mind or my heart."

It was then that I noticed that every time he would mention Chris, he would put his hand on his heart.

He looked us right in the eyes and said, "I was a fifteen-year-old coward and I murdered your son, and I'm sorry."

As he said the words, it looked like he dropped a ton of weight from his shoulders, and he looked a lot lighter in his spirit.

He also told us about the courses he did in prison. He is a good artist. In fact, his dad is a tattoo artist and he trained him since he was a kid to take up the trade.

He also told us about how he won top prizes for his artwork in prisons.

Then we were invited to tell him what it was like for us, what it was like that night and everything we went through, seeing them laughing and even lying in court, and what it was like having to wait sixteen weeks to bury our son.

As we were speaking, he asked if he could say something. He looked us in the eyes and said, "No one told me you had to wait sixteen weeks to bury Chris. I am so sorry." And tears appeared in his eyes.

That portion of the meeting ended. Now is when everyone is invited to stay for a cup of tea/coffee and a sandwich, and the part of the meeting when there are no facilitators running the course and you can just talk to each other. As we were sitting down with our refreshments, I asked if he was working. He replied no. I wanted to know why he was out of work. He got a job on construction but was made redundant and is now unemployed.

I looked at him and said, "I can get you a job tomorrow and get you trained as a curator of art." He held his cup of tea and said, "Would you do that for me?" I nodded and replied, "Yes, I would."

The meeting finally ended. We all shook hands and we left first, and the three of us had smiles on our faces.

CHAPTER 13

MEETING STEPHEN

The year was 2012. Stephen was the eldest of the gang and the one Vi most feared, because he was the one who told the girl to leave Chris in the road. Even though we had already gone through a lot of mediation before we met Jack, we had to go through it all again. There were still risk assessments to be done and we had questions that needed to be answered before the meeting took place with Stephen.

The meeting was held in the basement of a community hall in Epsom Surrey.

As before, we arrived first and took our seat. Again, Sian and Lizzy, the CEO from the Restorative Justice Council, came with us as support.

The way to enter the room was to come down the stairs and turn left into the room. We were all seated at the back of the room, which was about fifteen feet from the door.

I sat there watching and waiting for Stephen to enter, then I saw his foot come around the corner followed by his whole body. I got up out of my chair and, just like I did with Jack, I opened my arms. Then all heaven broke out. He didn't walk toward me; he ran and fell into my arms and cried on my shoulder like a baby. He kept saying, "I'm so sorry, I'm so sorry," and every time we let go, he would grab me again. This went on for what felt like ten minutes. As I write this, I can still smell his aftershave and tobacco.

We finally let go of each other. I think I was crying more than him.

Stephen then ran over to Vi and held her so tight I thought he was going to suffocate her.

It took a while to get him to settle down. As he took his chair he was trembling and crying.

(This was the young man who wanted to meet us but was prevented by professionals getting in the way.)

When he calmed down, he started to talk about his part in the fight. He regrets to this day telling the girl to leave Chris in the road.

Vi asked, "What did you think was going to happen? You left Chris unconscious in the road and you and the others just ran and left him to die."

I then said, "Did you think that he would get up after being kicked and stamped on? What did you think would happen to him lying in a busy road?"

At this point he couldn't look us in the face.

All he kept saying was, "I'm so sorry, I'm so sorry," and tears were rolling down his face. I have never seen so much remorse in all my life. He went on to tell us his part in the murder and again he has asked us to keep this private, which we have to respect.

The meeting went on for four hours. Just like the meeting with Jack, there were a lot of questions answered.

And then he asked, "How is Philip?" We invited Phil to all the meetings but he said he didn't think he could control himself, so we suggested, "Maybe you would like to give him a letter telling him what it was like for you."

Phil jumped at this and he composed this letter:

Stephen,

I have often thought if I got the chance to write or meet you what I would say. First of all, I hope the past eleven years have not been as kind to you as they have been for me.

I don't wish to dwell on ill feelings toward you but wish to inform you of what your actions have done to my life.

I do hope, though, that through all that has happened, you have looked inside yourself and found out what a foolish and destructive person you were.

I could not begin to tell you how it felt to have someone so close ripped out of my life and to have the future I would have had altered from what it should have been.

It has been a hard road these past eleven years. The worst thing for me is my children will never know what an amazing guy Chris was. It is my hope you continue to grow away from the coward you were that night into a decent person, not the mindless thug, animal you were.

Although I have a deep-rooted repulsion for your actions, I do forgive what you have done. I can separate the person from the action. You will never know of the haunting nightmares that plague me, especially near the anniversary, as I will never know what haunts your dreams too.

The one thing that has kept me going is my family. I will not let them down by becoming consumed with rage and bitterness that you and your friends inflicted on me.

To end this on a positive note, the one thing I want for you is to help others overcome the same situations you were in. This way you will honor the memory of my brother and help his legacy and stop foolish young men like you were throw their lives away, and their victims as well, as I realize you are as much a victim of your crime as Chris and I were.

With hope for your future,

Phil Donovan

The thing that pops out of the letter is when Phil says to Stephen, "Although I have a deep-rooted repulsion for your actions, I do forgive what you have done. I can separate the person from the action."

These are very strong words.

The meeting ended and while we were having tea and coffee I asked how his wife was. "I divorced her long ago," he said. "I now have a new partner and we're going to have a baby soon. We had a scan and it's going to be a boy."

(When the baby was born we got him a card and a toy, which we gave to Stephen's probation officer to pass on for us.)

I also asked him to come to Christopher's grave as I think he should say sorry to him.

(I asked the same thing of the other two, but to this day they never had the courage to do this.)

He said yes, he would do this. The meeting ended. There were more hugs and we all seemed to be on a high. Lizzy asked if we would drive her to the railway station. we were only too happy to.

In the car we were still on a high. As we got near the station I said to Lizzy, "I can't go home after what just happened. I will drive you home. Where do you live?" She argued, "No, it's too far. I will get the train," but in the end I won the argument saying, "I need to drive. I just can't get over what has happened." Lizzy then added, "But I live around 55 miles away."

The drive was something we will never forget. When we got to her house Lizzy invited us in for a cup of tea.

As she was turning the key, her husband appeared on the other side of the door. He said hello and then asked if we were hungry and would beans on toast be OK? We all started to laugh because this was the only normal thing that happened that day.

STEPHEN'S LETTER

About three weeks later, we were speaking to over six hundred probation officers for Surrey and Sussex, in a theatre just outside Brighton.

We were sitting in the foyer when Stephen's probation officer came up to us and said, "Stephen heard you would be speaking today and wanted me to hand this letter to you and ask if you would please read it."

So we sat there reading the letter to ourselves and she said, "No, he wants you to read it to everyone at the conference."

So we agreed to this and read it about twenty times to make sure we got it right.

This is the letter Stephen composed for us to read:

My name is Stephen Andrews and I along with other associates was involved in the death of Christopher Donovan on May 26, 2001. I was subsequently charged, convicted of murder, and given a life sentence.

During the first couple of years I found it too difficult to accept what I had done and fought against the sentence I received. I was approached to become involved with restorative justice at that time but I was not ready and the thought of meeting Christopher's family was something I could not contemplate. I was scared. However, as time went by I began to realize that in order to move on in my life I had to face up to the death of Christopher, take responsibility for the person I was then, and try and develop myself to lead a more positive life in the future.

I started to approach courses with a greater motivation; I wanted to understand and make changes.

I found the more I took responsibility, the better I felt inside.

I worked through my sentence and was able to develop my skills by completing education and trade courses as well as completion of offending behavior programs.

I was released in December 2011 and again given the opportunity to get involved with restorative justice.

I discussed this with my probation officer, Samantha, and she agreed to be my support.

Together we were in touch with the charity who acts as mediators throughout the process. I continued to feel very anxious about this mostly because I did not want to cause the family any more hurt or pain.

Despite fearing that they would think of me as a monster, I felt Ray and Vi wanted to meet me. It was the very least I could do to demonstrate my regret and remorse for what happened to Christopher and acknowledge the impact upon them and their family.

Despite my fears the meeting with the mediators reassured me and helped me to find the [courage] to meet Ray and Vi.

During the preparation meetings we exchanged messages and I knew about some of the questions before the face to face contact. One of the things they wanted me to know before we met was that they felt no anger and this really helped me to relax and prepare to face them.

I too was able to pass on to them that I wanted them to feel free to ask anything.

All our meetings with the mediators and then the final contact with Ray and Vi were held in a neutral place and was quiet, which seemed to help too.

At all times the mediators made it clear that it was a voluntary process and I knew that if it got too much I could withdraw. The meeting itself was amazing, emotional and went so well. It exceeded all my expectations in so many ways. Some of the questions were very difficult about the offense and what happened to Christopher, but I understood and respected why Ray and Vi need to know.

Hearing the family's experience at the time of Christopher's death, and the impact of losing him in such a horrible way, made it real and I was able to hear and see their pain for myself.

Being part of the restorative justice process and meeting Ray and Vi Donovan was more powerful than any victim awareness course and something that I will remember and no doubt influence the rest of my life.

It also gave me the opportunity to apologize to them for their loss and give some background to my own experiences and what I have done since.

When Ray and Vi told me they forgave me it meant everything. It meant that they understood that what happened to Christopher was an incident that never should have occurred.

Hearing them give me permission to have the best life that I can made me feel like a human again, a good person with a clear focus and a positive future. I owe that to Christopher. Meeting Ray and Vi has helped me to accept that I owe it to myself too.

When I committed this offense I was lost with no direction of purpose. That is no longer the case.

RAY

There is a sentence that has always stuck out and still does every time we read it. It's when Stephen says,

> **"WHEN RAY AND VI TOLD ME THEY FORGAVE ME IT MEANT EVERYTHING."**

It wasn't going to prison or doing a victim awareness course. It was sitting in a room with us and hearing for real the damage he did to our family.

A couple of years after the meeting, the Ministry of Justice invited us to do an interview about restorative justice on live national TV. A couple of days after the show Stephen's probation officer phoned to say Stephen's partner had handed her a card and ask if we would accept it. We said yes and the card was mailed to us.

Here is what his partner wrote to us:

To Ray and Vi,

It's hard to know what to write as I'm not very good with words, but just want to say thank you very much for your lovely gift and card. It was very kind of you to think of our son.

Seeing you both on the Daybreak program I was able to put faces to your names as I never knew before. It was quite emotional for me to watch, knowing it was Steve who did that to your son and took Christopher away from you.

I don't know how you find the strength and courage in your heart to forgive Steve for what he did but I am so very grateful that you have.

I know it doesn't make it any easier to deal with but Steve has turned his life around and is a good person now. He's a great dad, puts others before himself and is a hard worker. I can't even come close to imagining what you have been through but I am so sorry you lost your son.

Love, Donna

CHAPTER 14

MEETING RYAN

We met Ryan on March 3, 2013.

Again we had to go through months of mediation, and the meeting was set up in South Croydon in London.

Again Sian was with us along with another friend, Darren Way, founder of Streets of Growth.

Again we waited for Ryan to enter the room, and as he walked in I again stood there with open arms. He walked up to me unsure what to do. He then accepted my hug and went over to Vi to hug her. I noticed his father was in the room too. Looking around the room I asked Ryan, "Where is your probation officer?"

His father answered, "I am his probation officer," then we all took our seats and Ryan started to tell us about the events that happened that night.

He told us about how some of them went to meet a drug dealer and buy some drugs, and how they were just being a nuisance in the community that evening, and how they all crashed a party one of their aunts was having. In fact, they were so rowdy that she had had enough and made them all leave. As they left the building, two of them tried to steal a motorbike but couldn't start it.

Then they started to walk. At first they were becoming a nuisance shouting and making a ruckus and annoying the community and then they started to walk toward Chris, Phil, and Richard.

He went on to describe what happened as the boys came toward them:

We opened up to let them pass through but one of us sucker-punched Phil in the face and I saw the blood running down his face and I saw him pass out and fall to the ground. It was then some of us started kicking him in the head, and Chris came to help his brother, then myself and two others got Chris on the ground and kicked and stamped on his head. I don't know what happened. We just went crazy; we were like wild animals.

Then I remember someone shouting, "Leave him alone, the police are coming," and everyone started to run, but one girl went to get Chris off the road. But Stephen said something like, "Leave him there," and they both ran.

I was the last one standing there. I heard Chris moaning and I thought he was OK and would get up, so I gave him a couple more kicks in the head and face. He started to moan again so I repeated the kicking, then the woman shouted, "You're going to kill him. Leave him alone. I called the police and they are coming."

I ran to the alley and hid and looked to see if he would get up, then I saw a car come over the hill and swerve to miss him. The second car came over the hill.

Then using his hands he demonstrated the headlights coming over the hill and the car going over Chris and pulling him down the road.

He then added, "I still thought he would get up."

Vi said, "How can you say that? Are you mad?"

Ryan looked us both in the face and said the reason he thought Chris would get up is because it works in video games.

Vi replied, "What kind of a fool are you to think you can use that as an excuse? We're not going to accept it."

"I am not using this as an excuse," Ryan answered. "I killed Chris. I own it and for that I am so sorry. But you both have to understand that when you add drink and drugs and these nasty video games, it's a recipe for disaster."

As with the others, we told him what it was like for us and our family on the night he killed Chris and what it has been like since.

He was unable to look us in the eye. He had his head bowed as he listened to us and took in every word we said.

Philip didn't write Ryan a letter. He asked us to relay this message: "I don't hate you, but I hate what you've done."

When I finished, he asked me to repeat it and then asked me to repeat it a couple more times which I did.

Then he got up out of his chair and shouted, "You're doing my head in. You're doing my head in. This isn't what I expected. How can you say you forgive me for what I did to your Chris? I'm unforgiveable."

We all managed to settle him down. He was handed a cup of tea and later he felt a lot better and was fit to go home.

After more tears and hugs, the meeting ended.

At the end of each meeting, I asked all three to come to Christopher's grave and apologize to him, because he is the real victim here.

The only one to do this was Stephen. A few weeks after our meeting with Stephen, his probation officer had arranged a date for the visit.

CHAPTER 15

VISITING THE GRAVE

It was a cold and wet day. In fact, it didn't stop raining all that morning.

Vi and I pulled up at the main gate inside the cemetery, and about ten minutes later Stephen arrived followed by his probation officer.

We then drove into the car park and walked to where Christopher was buried. His grave is the second to last in a row of about twenty graves.

I looked at Stephen and for the first time I noticed he had a bunch of flowers in his hands.

I told him where Christopher's grave was and watched him and his probation officer walk down past the row of other graves toward his.

The sad thing is, when you look at the other graves, everyone in that line had a life. They were aged from ninety-six to around seventy, but when you come to Chris's grave and look at his age you see eighteen. He didn't have a life compared to the other people in their graves.

As we watched Stephen get on his knees and lay his flowers by the headstone, I looked up to heaven and said, "God, You are asking too much today." And I said to Vi, "Let's go for a walk."

So we left them and walked around the graveyard and about twenty minutes later we returned. I looked at Stephen and told him this is how we live our lives in memory of him, and if Chris was standing here right now he would tell you to move on and make something of yourself.

Stephen replied, "I hear of all the work you do in schools and would love to help you in any way I can."

We both answered Stephen, "It would be too much for you hearing our story over and over. Come to think of it, every time we give a talk you are there with us."

Then he asked if he could come and pay his respects again.

We said of course he could. He thought for a couple of seconds and said, "What if there's someone here? I wouldn't want to hurt them."

I looked right into his eyes and answered, "Stephen, no one knows you from Adam. If anyone asks who you are, just say you are a friend. We can't change the past but we can all move into the future."

Then he took out his phone and showed us a video of his son and we showed him photos of our grandchildren.

There were more tears before we all left and went our different ways.

CHAPTER 16

PHILIP'S JOURNEY TO FORGIVENESS

One of the biggest things in my life now is knowing my wife and children will never know my brother. It really hurts me to have had that person ripped out of my life. It affects everything, like Christmases you don't have with that person. Then there's birthdays you can't share with that person.

And the birth of my son. I would have loved for my brother to have been there, supporting me when that happened. I remember it was a bittersweet feeling for me when he was born because I had my son, but I didn't have my brother there with me.

Mum and Dad were Christians before my brother was murdered. Early on my dad said, "You know, as Christians we need to forgive these people."

At that time I don't think I really registered what it meant. When it was explained to me why you forgive I just thought it was a lot of Christian nonsense, but a few months later we discussed it as a family.

At first I felt hurt because I felt it would be betraying my brother. I thought if we forgave them, that meant they hadn't done any wrong but I didn't understand what it meant to forgive.

Then it was explained to me that when you forgive someone it doesn't mean that you say it's OK. It's quite the opposite. It's saying that yes, you did me wrong, but I'm not going to hold it against you. It was so hard for me to grasp what it actually meant at the beginning.

But the more I thought about it, the more I did want to do it. I wanted to release myself from all the anger and bitterness. I wouldn't be where I am today if I didn't forgive because I don't like to think of myself as a bitter person. For my family's sake I'm glad I have forgiven, and I'm glad my parents talked to me about it and made me see that it was the right thing to do. Forgiving someone isn't letting them off, it's letting yourself off the hook. One of the hardest things for me was to forgive myself.

I forgave others but I couldn't forgive myself because I kept thinking, "What if I stood somewhere else? What if we didn't go down that road?" One of the hardest things for me to deal with was that my brother, before he was murdered, said to me, "Shall we get a taxi?" Usually I would have said yes because I hate walking and it was quite a distance, but this night it was a nice night and I thought no, you know, we'll walk it. I had just been paid from work and I had the money in my pocket. I keep thinking to myself, "If only we got a taxi." The hard thing you have to live with is the "what ifs?" You think, if only I had seen it coming I could have averted it. But there is nothing you can do.

I felt so angry I couldn't even go to his grave because I felt I let him down. He protected me on that night and I felt like I couldn't protect him. I have only been to his grave twice and every time it fills me with anger because I think I could have done more. Everyone tells me you couldn't have done any more but that doesn't stop you thinking it, and it doesn't stop you feeling it, and it doesn't stop you dreaming about it, and it doesn't stop you thinking about it every second of every day.

CHAPTER 17

GOD OPENS
NEW DOORS

A number of years ago we started to do charitable work in which we shared our story. People seemed to respond in powerful ways to hearing about how we lost Christopher and how we came to make our peace with that in our family. One day the phone rang and when I answered I heard, "Hello. I am Christopher and Philip's old Religious Education teacher. I'm calling to ask if you would be interested in supporting a new course that an organization called Prison Fellowship is running in prisons." She went on to say that the course is for the prison inmates and is called the Sycamore Tree. This is a victim awareness and restorative justice program. The course runs one afternoon a week for six weeks and is attended by about twenty inmates at a time. It is run in young offenders' institutions and in both women's and men's prisons.

I asked, "Why we would we want to do something like this?" And she replied, "The Sycamore Tree gives victims a voice." That was enough for me to be interested.

The name of the course—the Sycamore Tree—comes from the Bible story of the tax collector in Jericho named Zacchaeus. As you may know, Zacchaeus was skimming money for himself and making people pay more tax than they should. The course introduces the people participating to Zacchaeus' meeting with Jesus and how that meeting changed him. It goes on to explore how Jesus helped him to realize the wrong he was doing and how he then went on to make amends to the community. Throughout the course, the people who participate—the learners—work in large and small groups to learn about the ripple effects of crime and how crime impacts upon victims.

A unique aspect of this course is how in the third week of the course, one or two victims come in and tell their story to the learners. People always say Week 3 is the turning point of the course when the learners, maybe for the first time, hear a victim speak, freely and openly about the harm that was caused to them. But they don't stop there. The victim representatives will all have gone on to make their peace with their offender or offenders, very often through participating in restorative justice.

The learners then have to write in their course workbook about what they have heard and how they have responded to it. In Weeks 4 and 5 they learn more about taking responsibility and how to repair harm.

Week 6 is another significant moment. In Week 6 the course tutor from Prison Fellowship invites members of the public to join the session to represent the community. This is the day the learners will make their Act of Restitution. This is a powerful moment. The learners have been invited to prepare some way in which to make an Act of Restitution. Some will write a letter to their victim, some to their family. Others will sing a song, maybe one they have composed or written the lyrics for. Some will write a poem and others will make something to symbolize their wish to say they're sorry. These can be given to the victim representatives who came to share their story of harm and repair.

When we understood what was involved and how the course ran, we both agreed to take part. Someone from Prison

Fellowship came to visit us to explain more about the course. They told us how the course is faith-based but not faith-promoting and how every faith or non-faith can take part.

Over a month later we were invited to speak in a local women's prison. This was to be the first of many Sycamore Tree programs for us.

When we arrived at the prison we met the rest of the team, then booked in at the gatehouse and were all taken to the chapel. The Sycamore Tree usually runs in the prison chapel, led by a course tutor and assisted by a number of Prison Fellowship volunteers.

We sat there not knowing what to expect. We prayed and the tutor told the volunteers about how the day would run.

We were told we would speak for around thirty minutes, then the women started to come in.

About halfway through the afternoon, the tutor said, "I am now going to introduce you to Ray and Vi Donovan who are going to tell their story."

We went to the front and the women sat there looking at us. As we talked you could hear a pin drop.

Now we hadn't met Christopher's killers yet, so all we talked about was how Chris was killed and how we forgave the people who killed him.

There were a few women crying as we explained how Chris died and the impact it had on our family.

After our talk we sat in small groups to answer questions from the women. Many asked how Philip was and how the rest of the family were. We returned to the prison again for Week 6 to once again represent victims as the learners make their Act of Restitution.

This was powerful. We had never experienced anything quite like it ourselves. The prison governor was there too, along with some people from the local Council.

One woman got up to talk. For her Act of Restitution, she made a pot pipe out of a plastic drink bottle. She talked about how drugs had ruined her life and destroyed her family. She then asked for a pair of scissors and began to cut up the pot pipe saying, "This is the end of my drug habit."

The next woman had drawn a picture of herself inside a cell surrounded by bottles, saying, "I made this prison and today I am going to ask for help to try to break free from the poison of alcohol."

Other women also got up to say something and explain their Act of Restitution, and as each one talked their photo was taken. Then the prison governor got up to speak and he was smiling and started his talk by saying, "In all my years working in prisons, this is the first time I had a pot pipe, a pair of scissors, and a camera all in the same place and all in front of me." Everyone burst out laughing, a welcome release from the intensity of the emotion we had all just witnessed.

We went home that day different people because we had seen the power of God.

A few months later we were invited back again to talk on a different course. This happened a few times, and while this was happening the DVD that we had produced to tell our story was going out to all the courses up and down the UK.

Then our phone didn't stop ringing. As the word went out about our story, we kept getting invited to come and do the very first Sycamore Tree in many prisons.

Now we meet a lot of drug dealers who won't admit they have victims. We always say, "The boys who killed Chris that night were high on drugs and you dealers say you don't have victims. Well, here we are. Have a good look because someone like you sold drugs to them that night and because of someone like you our son is dead. If you don't like what you hear, come and talk to me in the break."

Once in Wandsworth Prison, a notorious prison in West London, this big built man came over to me during one of the breaks and said, "Me and you, in the corner."

I said, "OK, let's go."

I thought he wanted to confront me but he started to cry and said, "Ray, I didn't just sell them. I brought drugs into the country too. Maybe half the men in this room, no half the prison, are here because of me. I didn't realize the harm I was doing till you made it clear. Ray, I don't know my victims to say sorry to. What can I do?"

I looked up and tried to look him in the eye and said, "We will be returning on Week 6 to be a stand-in for your victims. You could say sorry to us."

As we became more familiar with supporting the Sycamore Tree program, both Vi and I, no matter what prison, always stand by the door on Weeks 3 and 6 and welcome the participants as they enter the chapel.

At the start of one Week 6, an inmate approached me and asked if he could talk to me in private. He then put his hand in his pocket and pulled out a brass plaque. (Timpson, the shoe repair company, teaches prisoners shoe repairs and engraving—but not key cutting!) On the plaque he had inscribed:

In Loving Memory of CHRISTOPHER gone but never forgotten

Loved by all Mum Dad and Family

He then asked, "Have I offended you?" I think this was because I had tears in my eyes. I just looked at him and all I could say was, "That is better than any award."

That plaque now has a position of honor. A friend of ours did a portrait drawing of Chris that hangs in our front hallway, and placed inside the frame is this plaque for everyone who comes to our house to see.

One day we were invited to Kingston Prison in Portsmouth. No one told us this was a lifer's prison. Vi and I did what we usually do: we met the men at the door of the chapel as they came in.

After our talk two men came up to us and said, "You welcomed us as we came in today. You even shook our hands." We said, "Yes, that's right. We do this in every prison." Then they asked, "Do you know what we're in prison for?" We said, "No, we never ask that question." They replied, "We are here for murder and you welcomed us. No one has ever done that before."

We really learned how important and powerful a simple handshake was to them that day.

After we did a third Sycamore Tree course at Kingston Prison, a young man came up to us and said, "I have wonderful news for you both." He went on to say that he saw something in us, a peace that he wanted, and so he had decided to become a Christian and wanted to study theology. He ended up working in the chapel and was the only inmate to be allowed a laptop to help him study.

In another prison the men wanted to do something to help raise funds for our charity. They organized a gym marathon, and the tutor of the Sycamore Tree for that prison said he would match pound for pound the money they raised, thinking they wouldn't raise more than about £50 (about $64).

But that day they raised over £300 (about $380)! The tutor had to approach his church to ask for help to keep his promise.

We had acted as victim representatives on Sycamore Tree courses at Kingston many times when we learned that the government intended to close the prison.

We were invited by the governor to visit the prison the day before it closed. This was a very sad time for us having seen so many lives change at this prison.

In August 2010 one event in a prison blessed us to overflowing and we will never forget it. The prison is Thorn Cross Youth Offenders Institute in Warrington.

We were invited to come and do the Sycamore Tree course and when it ended and we were getting ready to leave for home, the prison chaplain asked if we would stay for an evening event. He went on to say, "You both have a free hand to say whatever God leads you to say, and if you want to do an altar call, please feel free."

The Sycamore Tree was powerful and the young men were very responsive. After it ended we had to hang around the chapel till around 5:30 p.m., so when the event started we were a bit tired. Then the room began to fill up with the young offenders and officers, and even a deputy governor came to hear us speak.

We talked for over an hour and the young men sat and took in every word. We ended in prayer, and at the end of the prayer I felt bold and did an altar call but I didn't want to offend anyone, so I said, "Please close your eyes." Everyone closed their eyes and I then said, "If you asked God into your lives, open your eyes."

Now throughout our talk the chaplain was sitting to the left of us. As I asked them to open their eyes, he jumped up and shouted, "We don't do this in this prison!" I thought, "Lord, I blew it. That's it. We won't be coming here again."

Then he walked over to where we were standing and shouted to the room, "How many of you have given their lives to Jesus?" And every hand but two went up.

He then said, "Right. Get up out of your seats and come to the front for prayer."

The young men all ran to the front and squashed us against the wall—it was so powerful.

We later found out that the two people who didn't put their hands up were already Christians.

Then after the prayer, one of the young men ran out and brought his friend, who had just finished playing football, into the chapel and asked us if we could tell him our story. We gave him a short account of what happened in our lives and he too gave his life to Jesus.

The prison governor, who had been standing at the back, said, "I only came in to meet you both, but as you began to talk I just couldn't leave."

The Head of Reducing Reoffending, a deputy governor said, "As you both were talking, my feet felt like they were stuck to the floor."

We have been invited back a few times to speak at the Sycamore Tree in this prison, then in 2011, during one of our visits, the chaplain asked if we'd do another Christian event again in the evening. We both said we would be only too happy to. That evening the young men came into the chapel and sat down and we were introduced. We gave our talk about what happened to us and how God got us through a terrible time. After our talk Vi did an altar call and around twenty-eight young men came forward and gave their lives to Jesus.

Once we were in HMP Bronzefield, a women's prison, and a woman came up to me and said, "You don't like me because you are a Christian and I am gay."

I asked, "What on earth ever gave you that idea?" She said, "Many so-called Christians have treated me like I am a leper." She went on to say she was abused as a child by her father and was kicked out of the army for fighting.

She then said something I will never forget. She said, "I don't have any mirrors in my cell because I am so ugly." I looked at her and couldn't believe what she just said. She was a very pretty young lady but people had put her down so many times that she started to believe them and lose all respect for herself.

I told her how pretty she was and to never believe what others say about you, and I even apologized for the way Christians had treated her.

I called Vi over and we gave her a hug.

Then on Week 6 this woman got up to speak. She said she now feels different about herself and she is sorry for hurting so many people. She looked at us and said, "Ray and Vi, thank you. I now have a mirror in my cell and look in it every day."

In HMP Winchester, a men's prison in Hampshire, after we told our story on Week 3 a man came over to me and said, "I don't know how you forgave them. When I get out of here I am going to find the man who killed my brother while I was in here and when I find him I am going to kill him."

After a prayer to ask God to give me the right words, I looked at him and said, "Tell me about your brother." He went on to talk about him, his likes and dislikes, and so on. As he was speaking about his brother, a smile came to his face.

I then stopped him speaking and said, "You are the most selfish person I have ever met. That smile on your face is good memories of your brother shared by you and your family. Not only that, but the moment you kill that person you will make more victims like you, and all the good memories will be gone because you will end up back here and your mother will have lost two sons." To be honest I thought he was going to hit me, but he just walked away.

When we went back for Week 6, and it was this man's turn to make his Act of Restitution, he went to the front.

His wife and mother were there to support him. He started to and tears came. He said, "I wasn't going to come to the front but I felt I had to." Then he began to talk about his brother and when he finished he looked at me and said, "Ray, you're right. Killing that man won't solve things, so I have changed my mind and moved on, and I will support my family so they and my brother will be proud of me."

After the meeting I went over and gave him a hug and said, "I thought you were going to hit me the other day." A smile came to his face and he answered, "Ray, I had to walk away. If I didn't I would have knocked you out for the count. But I thank you for opening my eyes and making me see sense."

It is not uncommon for us to hear the Sycamore Tree learners say something along the lines of what one man said: "I learned more in an hour about victim awareness from hearing Ray and Vi's story than all the courses I did in prison over the past eight years."

Once we were asked to speak as victims of crime for the Sycamore Tree in HMP Holloway, a women's prison in North London.

There were around twenty women prisoners on the course who listened to our story. We could tell they were moved as we talked. They were listening intently and dead quiet. After our talk some of the women were even crying.

But nothing could prepare us for what happened on Week 6 of the course.

Many women who went forward to make their Act of Restitution expressed deep remorse for their crimes.

One of the volunteers who was helping a young woman asked me if I wouldn't mind reading her letter for her to the room, as she was quite anxious.

I said yes, I would, but only if she felt able to stand next to me. She agreed and so we went out together to the front of the room and she stood a little behind me. I began to read her letter out loud.

About halfway down the paper I realized that this was a letter to the mother of a baby she had killed. In the letter she poured her heart out, being filled with remorse. It was so emotional. After I finished reading her letter I turned around to her. She had her head down and couldn't look at me but said, "You must hate me now." She put the hood of her jacket over her head and face and still wouldn't look up, such was the shame and guilt haunting her.

Well, by the grace of God I took her hand and told her that it was not true that I hated her and that she was loved and cared for.

We learned later that she gave her life to Jesus. All praise goes to the Lord. We both hope that God will also restore the mother of the child as well.

There was also a time we visited Greenock women's prison. This is on the west coast of Scotland.

We were asked to give an evening talk to a group of women who were doing a victim awareness course put on by the chaplaincy.

The room was set out with tables and chairs and when the women entered they all found somewhere to sit.

I said, "Let's split and sit at different tables." So I went to one and Vi went to another. The meeting started with tea and cakes and biscuits, which were already laid out on the tables.

Unfortunately, Vi had to pick the table with one of the hardest women in the prison. As she sat at the table and listened to them, it became apparent that this lady was the boss and she picked up the plate with cake and biscuits and passed them around the table. She did not offer Vi any and put the plate down and turned her back on Vi, leaving Vi in no doubt that she wasn't welcome.

Vi tried to chat to a few of the women at the table but she could see they were being manipulated by this lady.

Well, we were invited to come to the front and tell our story, and as we were speaking Vi glanced over to the table where she had been sitting and this lady had bowed her head. When we had finished we went around the tables to speak to the women and answer any questions they had.

When Vi reached the table where she had been sitting, the lady who wouldn't offer her a biscuit and had turned her back on her came over and sat next to her. She hugged her and said she was so sorry for her attitude. It was an instant change in her face. Where there had been rage in her eyes there was now peace.

CHAPTER 18

WHAT IS RESTORATIVE JUSTICE?

Restorative justice is a different way of tackling crime, based not on punishment but on healing the harm that's been caused.

It brings offenders into face-to-face conversation with their victims—and sometimes that dialogue is so powerful it can transform the future of each participant.

Victims can get answers to questions about the crime they've suffered, which for many brings new peace of mind. The person who committed the crime gets the opportunity to try to make amends to the people they've hurt. This has been shown to reduce future reoffending; restorative justice is used as an alternative to criminal prosecution (for lower level crime) but mostly it's used alongside the criminal justice system.

An important principle is that the participants should come to the restorative justice meeting voluntarily. No one should be forced to take part.

We at the Chris Donovan Trust believe very strongly that the facilitators should be properly trained and accredited, so that the encounter only goes ahead after thorough preparation of all parties, and an assurance of safety and total confidentiality.

—**SIAN WEST**, SECRETARY AND TRUSTEE
OF THE CHRIS DONOVAN TRUST

RESTORATIVE JUSTICE

Today's justice system is called "retributive justice," which asks:

- What crime has been committed?
- Who is to blame?
- What is the punishment?

This is all about revenge. Lock them up and throw away the key. But the person missing from this is the victim.

Now restorative justice also has three questions:

- Who's been hurt?
- What are their needs?
- Whose responsibilities are they?

Restorative justice puts the victim in the center of the justice system.

Restorative justice is not rocket science. It is just two people in a room talking.

Meeting the people who killed Chris was so positive and powerful for us. For the first time in years we felt we had a voice.

We were able to express our thoughts and feelings to the offenders and receive answers to questions that we were not able to ask in court. All too often in the court system the victims and family are rarely asked anything unless they are giving evidence. They are made to sit in the public gallery or in the well at the back of the court as spectators, nothing more. Sometimes you are invited to write an Impact Statement, which may not be read out in the court, and your feelings may not be relayed to the offender, as happened in our case.

When people see a restorative justice meeting on TV, it looks like it is put together in a very quick fashion, which is not true. It can take months of mediation meetings until the mentors feel the time is right for a face-to-face meeting to proceed.

For the parties to meet is completely voluntary on both sides and anyone can walk out if it gets too hard to handle.

The meeting place will have two rooms, one for the meeting to take place and the other to be used as a "time-out" room if anyone needs a break, or finds something too hard to hear and needs a bit of time out.

Both sides can bring someone to act as a supporter. They can participate, and even be involved in the preparation, but even if they do not speak, they can be a great help.

When we met the three young men who took Christopher's life and were able to tell them what it was like for us and our family, the things we had to go through and are still going through, and were able to tell them about the ripple effect and how it affected everyone from our family to the community, it made them realize the number of people who were affected by their actions.

Then to hear them tell the truth and admit their crime and say they were sorry made us both feel like a ton of coal was taken off our backs.

WE FELT FREE FOR THE FIRST TIME BECAUSE WE GOT ALL WE EVER WANTED: WE GOT ANSWERS TO OUR QUESTIONS AND THE TRUTH. NOW WE HOPE WE CAN LEAVE THOSE QUESTIONS IN THE PAST AND MOVE ON INTO THE FUTURE.

Why did it take all these years for us to meet these people and hear and see their remorse? Going over and over this won't bring back Chris, but we have hope, knowing these boys now understand what they did to us and our family and hopefully will not commit another crime and make more victims.

CHAPTER 19

RESTORATIVE JUSTICE TOUCHES OUR LIVES AGAIN

It was 2011 when we first met Roger. I was in HMP Wormwood Scrubs, a prison in West London. It was Week 6 of the Sycamore Tree and Roger was there as a representative of the community. (Vi was with me on Week 3, but she couldn't make it to Week 6 because she was speaking in another prison that afternoon.)

It was a powerful meeting. All the inmates went to the front and made Acts of Restitution and again a few wanted to meet their victims to apologize after hearing our story.

The course ended. The men went back to their landings, and it was time for us all to leave. It was then that our friendship with Roger started when out of the blue he came over and invited me to go for a bite to eat. While we were in the restaurant I asked him to tell me his story.

ROGER'S STORY

Roger is an ex-policeman and coroner's officer.

Roger's house had been broken into twice. One burglary was

while he and his wife, Jane, were asleep and the other burglary was when his wife came back from taking a friend out to the park and found the front door open and lights on in the house. The ripples of that second burglary were that Jane just couldn't stay in the house on her own anymore. So every morning on his way to work Roger would drop Jane off at a friend's house and pick her up later when returning from work.

And not long after the last burglary, Roger had to go through the trauma of losing his beloved Jane who went to be with the Lord in 2007.

A few years later Roger was sitting in his living room watching TV. It was around 11:30 in the evening when his doorbell rang. Half asleep he got up from his chair and went to the front door, thinking it must be a neighbor or somebody in need. As he opened the door he saw two hooded men standing on his porch.

Thinking quickly, he put his foot at the bottom of the door as they tried to push into his house.

The next thing that happened was the door opened a few inches and a hand came through. A gun was being pointed an inch away from his left temple. He began to shout that he was being burgled by armed men. There was a struggle. Roger was able to keep the door from opening further and, fortunately for him (he didn't know it at the time), there were people walking down his road who disturbed the two men on his doorstep.

Suddenly the hand holding the gun was whipped out and he slammed the door shut. He ran into his dining room and waited for a while. He was afraid that the men would shoot through the frosted glass in the door. After what seemed like a lifetime but must have been only a matter of a few minutes, he poked his head around the door to see if the men were still there.

When he saw there was no one, he rushed into his front room, picked up his phone then went upstairs to his bedroom while calling the police. His bedroom had a bay window and he could look out onto the street to see if the men were visible.

He told the police that armed men had tried to break into his house. The police call handler kept talking to him on the phone while they alerted the local police force.

When the police arrived, he spent over three hours with them, totally shattered and emotionally drained. The following Sunday he went to church and when he got home there was a message on his phone asking for him to contact the detective in the case as soon as possible. He called the number and the police said they had arrested a man and recovered two guns.

Roger felt deeply affected by what had happened, but as a Christian what was he to do?

He could just ignore it and let the justice system take its course. He could wait for the offender to go to court and be sent off to prison. Somehow he just could not do that. It wasn't within him because he knew he had to forgive the guy who held the gun an inch away from his head.

So, he wrote a letter to the judge.

In the letter he wrote that he was a volunteer at the chaplaincy in Wormwood Scrubs prison and he had seen people go on the Sycamore Tree course and had their lives totally transformed.

He therefore asked for two things. First, that he could have justice with mercy. He said he was clear that the man had committed a serious offense and he knew that a prison sentence would be passed. But he wanted the judge to give him justice with mercy.

The second thing he asked the judge was to put the offender on a Sycamore Tree course, so he could actually learn the effects crime have, not only on the victim, but the community too. All the people on his street were afraid to open their doors after the incident.

The third paragraph of the letter he addressed to the offender directly. He told him he would never, ever forget the trauma of that night, but he had forgiven him and he had wiped the slate clean. He held nothing whatsoever against his name and that if he was willing to meet personally then Roger would tell him face-to-face that he had forgiven him.

The police officer in charge of the case said, "What on earth are you doing, Roger? I'm trying to get this man put away. He is a violent criminal."

Roger answered, "I have no choice because, being a Christian, forgiveness is not an occasional extra. Forgiveness is a command."

Roger then went on to tell me how the case was heard while he was in New Zealand, so he never got to say what he felt. He also talked about how the police found four more guns in the offender's garage but they were fake.

We met up a few more times and one day I asked if would he like to meet the offender. Roger jumped off his seat and shouted, "Yes, I sure would!"

We contacted a charity and he met the facilitators who were going to do the mediation before the actual meeting. After a few months they got the ball rolling. The meeting was to be held in a prison in Devon, about a four-hour drive from where Roger lived.

I was on the phone a week before the meeting, asked if he was OK about everything and if anyone was going with him. He answered no, he will be okay. He planned to drive to the prison and after the meeting he would find a hotel, stay overnight, and drive back the next day.

I warned him it would be emotionally draining and it would be unsafe for him to drive that far and then return. I offered to drive him there and back, and he agreed.

On the day of the meeting we set out early in the morning. When we arrived at the prison we met the facilitators, and we were all escorted to the chapel.

After a few minutes the offender walked in, shook everyone's hands and then sat down. The facilitator asked if he would like someone to be at the meeting with him, but he answered, "No. I'm OK, thanks."

The meeting started and Roger had chosen to speak first. He told the offender about all he had been through with the break-ins and losing his wonderful wife, Jane, "and then you turn up at my door and shatter me." He also talked about the effects that night had on him and the nightmares that are ongoing, how he jumps at any sound in his house, and every night he sees someone standing at the foot of his bed with a gun.

It was now the offender's turn to talk. He told us about his life and his childhood and how he spent most of his life in prison and his involvement in gangs.

"Your house was the wrong house. We were after a gang leader that a drug dealer wanted punished. It was your posh voice that saved you."

The meeting took about two hours, but one of the facilitators turned to me and asked if I had something to say.

I answered, "Yes, I have a question for Roger."

Roger looked at me as if to say, "What's going on?" I then said to Roger, "From the first time we met you kept saying the gun that was put to your head was a replica. Is that right?"

Roger answered, "Yes. Why are you asking me this now?"

Looking at him I said, "You didn't hear what he said, did you?"

He said, "The only reason I didn't kill you was your voice."

I then turned to the young man. This was a moment of truth. He answered that it had been a real gun and yes, Roger's voice had saved him.

There were a lot more things said at the meeting that have to remain private, but it was a powerful meeting.

The meeting closed and Roger got out of his chair and asked the young man if he would stand up. The young man seemed uncertain because it looked like no one had given him a hug for a long time.

We then all had a cup of tea and a general discussion. The offender told Roger he was older than he thought. Roger replied it had been "great meeting the other 99 percent of you, having only seen your arm."

The whole day was amazing. It had started with Roger feeling apprehension. Before the meeting the offender had sent Roger a message saying he was an evil man, but Roger saw good in him.

And Roger's prayer was that good will grow in him and, thanks be to God, that his whole outlook on life would change for the better.

Then it was time for us to leave. Anyone who knows me and Roger knows that when we are together we can talk for hours, but on the drive home Roger hardly said a word. Every now and then he would say, "Ray, it was real," and then holding his thumb and index finger with a small gap between them he said, "I was that near to death!" This went on for the four-hour drive home. We were near Roger's house in London about ten o'clock at night and we both realized that we had had nothing to eat all day. Luckily, Roger knew a pub that would still serve food that late.

I then dropped Roger off and drove home. I was amazed at the power of forgiveness I witnessed that day.

Roger says now about restorative justice, "I would recommend restorative justice as it not only gets you the answers you need to hear, it also helps stop the repeating nightmares."

God bless you.

Roger has been the chairman of the Chris Donovan Trust since 2011.

TESTIMONIES

We would like to thank Restorative Justice Gloucestershire for giving their permission to include these stories.

LOUISE'S STORY

I went home one day and the window was missing. I noticed the curtain was blowing. That's when I knew I'd been burgled. I went into my own bedroom and could see all the drawers had been pulled out. I was more shocked than anything else.

When the police asked me what happened, I had no idea what was gone.

You forget things in your house but I pictured things missing over time. After the police left me, Victim Support called and I talked to them on the phone.

Soon after Sarah, a Restorative Justice volunteer facilitator, contacted me.

Knowing that someone had been in my house made it feel dirty. He'd been through my belongings. The impact on my daughter was bad. Afterward she woke up in the night, worried about him coming back.

Sarah helped me a lot. When I said I wanted to meet the offender, Sarah told me what the room for the restorative justice meeting was going to look like, and what to expect.

He came in and apologized and I asked my questions. He offered to pay back the cost of the things he took. I wanted to know if he would still be around my area.

It was a useful experience. I didn't know what he looked like but he knew what I looked like from the photographs in my flat.

William, the offender, wrote my daughter a letter saying he was not coming back. That helped her. She used to wake up and after she got the letter she got over it. I've got used to it too now; I used to double-check all the windows and doors all the time. The timing of the meeting was just right. Not too close to the burglary. I had time to think about it.

I would say definitely go for it. You can ask the offender what you want until you get answers. You can tell if they are genuinely sorry or just saying it. It changed my opinion of him.

WILLIAM'S STORY

It was always thought I was going to be in trouble. I was inquisitive and naughty, which led to me being angry and malicious. I was in and out of prison and bail hostels. Another prisoner called Lewis told me about restorative justice. I was ready to change but not sure how to.

A leopard can't change its spots overnight. It is a long process but I knew I could change. I needed something to trigger it, and it was the restorative justice conference for me.

The fact that there was a little girl involved who was traumatized was even worse. That made me think of my partner's little girl. I spent time thinking about questions I wanted to ask. I thought I was ready but I was absolutely petrified. I got to the door and I didn't want to go in. Sarah, the volunteer, encouraged me.

I couldn't look at Louise but got asked to look at her when I told her what happened. That was the hardest thing I've ever done in my life. I tried to explain everything to her.

She told me about her day and why she was not at home. Louise said her elderly parents had been burned in a house fire and both were hurt. She was at their house then she got back with her daughter. She had nightmares and refused to go back to live in the house. That really got to me. To wreck that little girl's life…I really understood it because of what had happened to me.

I made Louise aware that I was sincere when I asked questions.

"Do you want to know where I live, if I drink?"

"What if you see me in the street?"

"Do you want me to cross the road or acknowledge you?"

"Can I pay back the damage?"

She needed to know who the other person was. She didn't know who they were and wanted to know if she could end up sitting next to them on the bus.

The shame I felt in that room that day was nothing compared to court.

Louise asked me to write a letter to her daughter—from the "bad man." That had a big impact on me to be called "bad man." It took me two to three weeks to write. I found that really hard because I had always thought of myself as lovable rogue but I realized I was not—I was a bad man!

I came out of prison eleven months ago and my license has finished. It is the longest time I have been out and not committed a crime. I have also had restorative justice training and am now a volunteer. I've had the support of a police sergeant in Cheltenham too, including help finding employment.

> THE MORE THINGS YOU DO WRONG,
> THE MORE YOU SUPPRESS YOUR CONSCIENCE.
>
> RESTORATIVE JUSTICE HAS GIVEN ME
> BACK MY CONSCIENCE.

Now I can't do anything without thinking of what it will do to someone else. For instance, when I was walking back from the dole [unemployment] office with some lads, I stopped one lad from stealing a pint of milk. I would recommend restorative justice to anyone; it's life changing.

ALICE'S STORY

I became aware of the burglary when I returned home from work one afternoon.

As I unlocked the front door I noticed some empty bags on the hall floor and the cupboard door was open. The back door was open and the lounge window had been forced open. Both upstairs and downstairs had been searched with discarded items and drawers open. My grandmother's ring had been stolen from its box along with my husband's iPhone. The most upsetting thing was the theft of a large, heavy metal box inlaid with mother of pearl. It didn't contain anything of value but was full of sentimental and irreplaceable items. This was the item I most wanted back.

My husband was also away on the day of the crime and that added to my distress.

My husband and I were somewhat frustrated that our attempt to attend court was thwarted by Leonard's (the burglar's) illness and we were both happy to meet with him to talk about what happened. Therefore, when we were approached by a Restorative Justice volunteer, we were keen to proceed.

We chatted about the format of the conference with a volunteer and they left their contact details so that a suitable date could be arranged for the conference. I write children's books and I have also visited the prison library to donate books. I also wanted to give books to Leonard's three-year-old daughter as part of the repair process.

My husband and I asked several probing questions and also explained how much the burglary had distressed us both; this really hit a chord with Leonard. He apologized sincerely several times and said that he would never carry out a burglary again. He aimed to improve his life for himself and for his three-year-old daughter.

During the process I felt well-informed and overall the process exceeded my initial expectations. Overall, I had a positive experience of restorative justice and would recommend it to others.

LEONARD'S STORY

I spoke to a Restorative Justice facilitator in HMP Gloucester who explained all about the restorative process. After discussing the crime with the facilitator, I realized just how many had been affected by my actions, the victims and their family and myself and my family. I realized the householder would feel violated, scared, and assume that I might go back. Even though it was hard, I decided that I wanted to participate in a restorative justice conference.

I would say I didn't mean to hurt them, cause harm or fear. I would like a chance to try to explain. I could go a little way toward it, but can't repair the harm. At the beginning of the conference, I became quite defensive and wanted to know whether these questions were from the facilitator or from the victims. The facilitator assured me that this was the process that we had to go through and had to talk about what had happened.

After this initial tension, I started to open up and explain the day of the burglary. I had recently split up with my girlfriend and had been sleeping rough. I was very unwell with various medical conditions and on morphine and antidepressants.

JANE'S STORY

Our son was involved in a car accident where one of his friends was driving and the other was killed. Our son consequently suffered brain damage from the accident.

We first heard about restorative justice when we got a telephone call from a volunteer, Paul. Initially I said no. The incident was too raw and our son was still in and out of the hospital. At the time we had a lot on our plate and things were hectic.

Our family was falling to pieces and the last thing we wanted was to let outsiders in. After another phone call from Paul, we talked it over and I agreed. Paul highlighted that the process was completely voluntary and we could withdraw at any time. I researched a little bit more about restorative justice and was interested to see how it could help with our case.

The first meeting with the volunteers, Paul and Charlotte, was fantastic—it was the best thing we've ever done, even if nothing else came out of it and it didn't progress to a conference. We hadn't spoken much about the incident as a family, and during the meeting we all just talked and talked and talked!

Paul and Charlotte put a lot of work into making sure the conference went ahead and was safe. They were always available on the phone if needed.

I didn't feel any anger toward the offender, as he was a friend of my son, but I needed him to know what he had done to our family. This was why I wanted to progress with a conference.

The conference day was very nerve-wracking. It was the most frightening thing I had to do. I was very nervous to meet the person who caused the last fifteen months of hell. However, when we walked into the room he was a shadow of his former self; he looked so pale and had lost a lot of weight. I felt sadness and pity—he looked so ill. It reminded us that he was human too.

The conference was so useful because we were able to ask what we needed to ask. We all live together in a small town and we needed to know what would happen if we see each other in the street. This was so important because it was inevitably going to happen. It was decided that our son wanted no further contact with the offender.

Until you have participated in restorative justice you can't explain how powerful it is. You see the offender in a different light. It has had such an impact on our lives. It really was a fabulous thing—it has made such a difference. We have come out the other side so much stronger. We are able to move on with our lives. It's the best thing we ever did. I support it 100 percent and I think it should be available throughout the country.

DAVID'S STORY

I took part in the restorative justice conference just under twelve months ago. This was approximately fifteen months after the accident occurred.

I was driving back from a night out where I was the designated driver. I was speeding as I came down a hill and overtook a car on double white lines. I turned my head to tell one of the passengers to put his belt on and lost control of the car. It spun and hit a barrier, forcing the car to roll into an underpass. As the car rolled, one of the passengers was thrown out of the car and passed away at the scene.

The crime caused me to lose a lot of friends and it had a detrimental effect on my mental health; I had depression and started to drink and smoke.

Being sent to jail was a bad thing that happened but I turned it into a positive by gaining qualifications and sorting my life out. I am now back at college and have solid plans for my future and they are going well.

My experience of taking part in the restorative justice conference was good, but don't misunderstand me—it was the hardest thing I have ever had to do in my life. Although I am glad that I did—it gave me a chance to get my side of the story across to both sets of families instead of them just having the scientific evidence.

It also gave the opportunity to apologize to them. I would recommend the conference to other people, but I think they need to be strong enough mentally as it was an extremely hard thing to do, not just during the meeting, but afterward as well. I think it would help to show people with less remorse what they are doing to their victims and maybe help to prevent them reoffending.

I think that the way my conference was dealt with was as good as it possibly could have been, both before the conference and the aftercare.

I felt I was in a room with people I could trust and that it was a safe environment.

HMP GRENDON

HMP Grendon is a prison which runs as a democratic therapeutic community. All of the residents have applied to transfer to address their past experiences. Each wing is comprised of residents who have committed a range of offenses, who work together to address the difficulties they have had in the past in terms of relationships, emotional management, offense supportive attitudes, and self-management skills. Every interaction and event is taken as an opportunity to explore the past and how it may link to this. There are five wings, one for men with learning difficulties, one which specializes in those who have committed sexual offenses (although there are men throughout the establishment who have done so), and one which is the Enhanced Assessment Unit. Residents stay a minimum of 18 months but many stay for three to four years.

There had been a difficulty with those who had been gang members and how they integrated into the community and so the "Changing the Game" gang awareness program was introduced. Ray and Vi have attended the events marking the end of each program and spoken from the heart about the impact the loss of Christopher had on them. They are an integral part of the work at HMP Grendon. Each time they visit and make a speech they have a profound impact on all who hear them. My first experience of hearing them was through a victim awareness event on another wing. As a result we invited them to D wing to speak at a community meeting. The wing had to vote and agree for them to come, and in anticipation each person thinks about their own victim and the impact they had on them. This in itself was very powerful before they even arrived. When they came they sat on the wing of 40 men, who each spoke about who their victim was. It was very moving to imagine all of the named victims in the room. Ray and Vi then spoke about their experience with losing Chris, and the pain was palpable. Powerful feelings were evoked in the residents, who were able to express these on that morning and for many months afterward as they continued with their therapy. In the community room there are bricks on the wall where residents and staff leave their thoughts and Ray and Vi reiterated their usual message that no matter what you have been through in life and have done to others you are worthwhile. Their willingness to forgive is commendable.

As anyone who has heard them speak knows, they have a profound impact on all who hear them. They have since visited on many occasions and each time inspired more people to apply for the restorative justice process.

Ray and Vi contacted me about *The Listening Room*, a play which is a reenactment of a restorative justice conference performed by professional actors. The actual words from the conferences are used, and it includes those of Ray and Vi Donovan. We then raised funds for the play to be staged in HMP Grendon, and this happened on the first of December 2017. Ray and Vi attended and spoke of how they felt to see it performed. In addition, on the same day, staff from the Prison Radio Network held a discussion group with residents and recorded interviews with residents who had been involved in the gang lifestyle. This was broadcast on the Prison Radio Network, along with an audio performance of The Listening Room. Again this led to residents applying for restorative justice. Ray and Vi have touched so many people and helped them to deepen their feelings about their victims by their non-judgmental and caring approach to the residents at Grendon.

—**DR. GERALDINE AKERMAN**, THERAPY MANAGER, PHD,
REGISTERED FORENSIC PSYCHOLOGIST

VIEWS FROM RESIDENTS AT HMP GRENDON ON WHAT MEETING WITH RAY AND VI MEANT TO THEM

I took part in a gang awareness course called "Changing the Game" and at the end of it we had an end of course graduation. All of us who took part in it sat at the front facing the audience along with the course facilitators. There were also two other people there who I had never met before. I was sitting next to one of them, a very talkative, friendly and pleasant man who shook my hand when we met. I found out then that his name was Ray and he then introduced me to Vi.

The graduation went on. We all gave speeches about what we gained from the course, then we got presented with our certificates. It was a very happy, proud moment, in front of some of our probation officers and peers.

Then Ray and Vi got up and gave us all their story. I have been in prison for 13 years and this was the very first time that I had the opportunity to hear first-hand, face to face, the horrific, traumatic, devastating effects of the impact of a murder from a direct victim's perspective. Hearing their story hit me so hard. My heart felt heavy. I felt so guilty. I felt as if it was me who took their son's life. I could no longer look them in the eye, hearing the little details that I never even thought about as a person who had created victims myself; being told by the police that they could not touch their son, could not even kiss him or hold his hand because he was a "crime scene," not being able to bury their son until they finished their investigation, in the courtroom at the trial, having to sit right at the back of the room and having the people who committed the murder walk past them so close and hearing the jury ask, "Who are they?," hearing how the murder of their son affected their family life. Vi said that there was a time that she was so angry that her grandchildren did not want to be around her. All that was shocking to hear.

I went from feeling happy and proud to feeling sorry and sad. But I didn't stay feeling that way. I couldn't really understand how people who have gone through everything that they have could come into a prison where they knew that they are going to meet people who have made other families feel the way they feel, and be so friendly and pleasant when introducing themselves to me.

I am aware that I smile when I am feeling anxious, nervous, or uncomfortable, and I know I was feeling uncomfortable with my feelings at that event. I was feeling so bad for them for everything that they have experienced, and at the same time lifted that they were treating me with kindness after what I have done. I remember very clearly when the event was over and we were all saying our goodbyes Ray shook my hand again and said, "Keep smiling." I left the event feeling good.

The next time Ray and Vi made an impact on my time here at Grendon was when they attended the Victim Awareness event. Again they shared their story with us all but this time they spoke more about restorative justice. The biggest thing I took away from it was how they forgave the people who murdered their son. This was another thing that shocked and confused me. It made me see Ray and Vi as strong people. I couldn't even imagine how hard it would be to do that, but they said it felt like a weight was lifted from their shoulders and it helped them to move on with their lives.

That made me think about my victims and if they would want the opportunity to meet me and express their feelings to me and me to them. It made me think, "Do I deserve forgiveness? Do I want it?" And to answer those questions I think about the demonstration Ray made at the event. He took out a five-pound note and asked us how many Yorkie bars we can buy with this. Then he crumpled it up, put it in his mouth, chewed it up, spat it out, and then stamped all over it. Then he picked it up and asked us the same question again. How many Yorkie bars can you buy with this? What he was trying to tell us is that we all have value, no matter what we have been through and that we are all worth it.

So, to answer the questions, "Do I deserve forgiveness and do I want it?," after meeting Ray and Vi the answer to those questions is yes.

WHAT CHRISTIANS AND LEADERS ARE SAYING ABOUT *RESTORED AND FORGIVEN*

When I first heard Ray and Vi Donovan talk about their passion for restorative justice, I knew that they reflected the values of Restorative Justice International (RJI). Today the Donovans serve on RJI's Global Advisory Council and have appeared as guests on an RJI podcast because of their strong support of victim-driven restorative justice. As victims and survivors of a violent crime the Donovans are powerful witnesses for real systemic justice reform, because restorative justice is critical for victims to heal and to hold offenders accountable. Like RJI, the Donovans are strong advocates of in-custody restorative justice programs using crime victims and victim offender dialogue processes. Increasingly, crime victims worldwide are choosing restorative justice because it provides an opportunity to meet their offenders and get answers. By meeting the Donovans in person the offenders saw the direct impact their violent acts had on their victims (or victims' family) and thus encouraged them to take responsibility for their actions—something lacking in the traditional justice system. The Donovans could finally get answers to questions about their son's death, but restorative justice also opened the door to much more. Forgiveness can occur through restorative justice although it is not expected and victims should never be urged to forgive. If forgiveness does happen, as it did in the Donovans' lives, then a deeper healing occurs and all benefit. RJI is pleased to support the Donovans, and the Chris Donovan Trust, as they reach so many crime victims, offenders, and ex-offenders with the message of hope which restorative justice provides.

—LISA REA, PRESIDENT, RESTORATIVE JUSTICE INTERNATIONAL (RJI)
WWW.RESTORATIVEJUSTICEINTERNATIONAL.COM

I have been in awe of Ray and Vi Donovan since I first met them more than three years ago talking about their son Chris. In January 2015 I paid a visit to a now-defunct Sutton Youth Center to see how our local Council was engaging with young people and sat down to hear the Donovans tell their ill-fated story of Chris's last hours, the lives that were broken as a result of the life that was lost, and how it was so important to make clear choices to avoid gangs, weapons, and the crushing of aspiration that would likely follow.

The young people they spoke to hung on every word. I looked around at some teary eyes before realizing that mine were the same. Since getting to know Ray and Vi better, I have heard of the many schools and prisons where they have repeated this exercise. The vast majority of us will never have to experience the depths reached when a child is snatched from their family in such terrible circumstances.

But to turn this despair into such a positive movement is incredible and deserves celebrating.

This is a movement that the Donovans have started to nurture. Their annual awards event brings together small groups and individuals from around the country to showcase the work that is going on at a grassroots level. Attendees realize, sometimes for the first time, that they are not the only ones.

Just about all have incredible stories to tell, either as a victim, former gang member, or drug addict, who have channeled their energies into turning around young people's lives before it's too late. It's always a privilege to play a small part and just be in the room with so much love, energy, and mutual support. Ray and Vi are at the center of that every time, full of love.

Ray and Vi have shown a huge amount of courage, first in meeting those who killed Chris, then facing prisoners across the country to challenge them on their behavior and choices, and tackling decision makers about the greater use of restorative justice.

The pedestal that I am putting them on here is not apparent when one meets the down-to-earth couple at first. It doesn't take long to see their dedication, energy, and resolve shine through in the conversation.

People will leave with two new down-to-earth, jolly and loyal friends and an inspiring story which brings much-needed hope to a complex issue that has defeated policy makers and community leaders for so long.

—**PAUL SCULLY**, CONSERVATIVE MP FOR SUTTON AND CHEAM

Christopher Donovan's tragic, senseless death was one of the earlier cases into which I led the investigation. At that time I had less experience of how the recently bereaved reacted. Years later, when I had dealt with scores of murders, I was none the wiser.

There is no "correct" or normal way of responding to the loss of a loved one. Every family will take the dreadful news differently and the role for the police is consistent in that it is to support the family as best they can—but that will require different action in every individual case.

It was clear to us that Vi and Ray and Phil were utterly devastated but that their faith—and the support from their congregation—was to be their guiding light. The absence of anger or talk of revenge was striking.

When Christopher's murderers were convicted, the feelings I had are still with me. Vi and Ray were so grateful to me and my team and I was proud of that. Yet my overriding emotion was sadness that, for all we had achieved, despite us doing the very best we could, Christopher was still gone. I never, thereafter, speak of "closure" for families after a trial. I knew that, no matter how well the legal process went, their loss would never be forgotten.

Vi and Ray have managed, though, to create a real force for good from the desolation of Christopher being taken from them. They have channeled whatever emotions they had into spreading the word and showing the world that losses like theirs can be avoided. By their tireless campaigning they are ensuring that Christopher is helping others and changing lives just as I am sure he would have done if his life had not been cut so short.

These two decent and compassionate parents are of course most wonderfully unusual in how they have reacted and what they have done. They are always most complimentary about how my team and I dealt with their tragedy and I find it utterly humbling to have that level of regard from two such remarkable people. They have my complete admiration.

—**COLIN SUTTON**, FORMER SENIOR INVESTIGATING OFFICER,
METROPOLITAN POLICE

After Ray and Vi talked at my son's school, he came home and retold the gut-wrenchingly honest account of Chris's death, and the ripple effect it had on Ray and Vi and their other children. I was hooked.

I was hooked on their account of how, not only did they sit in the same room as the boys who murdered their son to get the truth behind the brutality of that night, but they hugged and forgave the murderers. How?

Their experience provoked so many conversations with my teenage sons, younger daughter, and husband about violence and forgiveness, about the ripple effects of petty crime, and drugs. I had to find out what made these parents get up each morning and retell the horror, day after day to people in schools, prisons, and churches. It changed my life and that of so many others. I rang them to say "thank you" for instigating such important discussion. Ray and Vi invited me round for a cup of tea and I ended up being their assistant for two years!

They have to be one of the most generous, inspirational couples ever.

They have dedicated their lives to trying to save others from going through, not only the pain they have suffered, but the pain they openly acknowledge the boys who murdered Chris have suffered.

—LINDA MADIGAN

I met Ray and Vi around two years after the tragic death of their son, Christopher, when the pain of his death and manner in which he died was freshly burned into their hearts and minds. Something about their experience, and their reaction to it, impacted my life—and I immediately knew that God was going to take them into places they would never have dreamed of going, where they would impact many thousands of people's lives as they shared their story with hurting people everywhere.

The Bible tells us that God Himself chose to send His only Son, Jesus, to die upon the cruel cross of Calvary to take the punishment for the wickedness of all mankind. As a result of the sacrifice Jesus made in laying down His life for us, God chose not to remember our sins any longer, but to banish them from His mind as far as the east is from the west.

Needless to say, Ray and Vi are not God—but I have always been aware that both of them make a daily decision, a choice, to forgive those who so callously murdered Christopher. They do this despite the pain and the loss they still feel—and they do it because they make a daily choice to show the love and the forgiveness of our heavenly Father to those they meet across the world—to the men and women who have a desperate need to receive the forgiveness that, in finality, only God can give.

Ray and Vi's story is an ongoing one. Their story will impact and challenge you as you read it. I hope and pray that as you do so, you will receive the love and forgiveness which God offers you today.

—**BILL PARTINGTON**, HEAD OF AFFILIATE DEVELOPMENT,
UCB RADIO

Just because you have failed doesn't mean you're a failure. You are worth it." When you're serving three life sentences for murder, attempted murder, and kidnap, those powerful words are hard to hear, difficult to believe, and very complicated to comprehend.

You may think that I came across these statements in a deep philosophical book or a self-help book, but I actually read them written in a black marker pen on the wall in D Wing's community room. Don't worry, it's not vandalism or graffiti. There is an actual place on the wall where residents who are moving on, staff members, and visitors to the wing write messages to other D wing residents. Those strong messages were written by two strong people, Ray and Vi Donovan. That was the first time they made an impact on me in my time at Grendon.

I have known Ray and Vi Donovan for ten years through their extraordinary work with the Sycamore Tree restorative justice course as well as prison-wide restorative justice victim impact events at HMP youth offending institution Thorn Cross where I have served since 2007 as senior Anglican Chaplain.

Ray and Vi have tirelessly spread their story of hope and restoration in prisons, schools, churches, on television and radio.

The brutal and unprovoked murder of their precious son Christopher would have destroyed the faith and very lives of most people; however, through their faith and stubborn will to forgive and bless the very people who had caused them such harm, they have become conduits of tremendous healing and transformation.

The very first victim impact event I experienced with Ray and Vi at Thorn Cross resulted in 53 young offenders making a formal response to the challenge to come forward and to publicly commit and apologize for their actions and commit their lives to Christ.

Every one of those young lives has been changed for God and changed for good. Ray and Vi have committed their lives to helping to bring healing to both victims and offenders through their dynamic faith and very powerful incarnation gospel of forgiveness.

Let Ray and Vi change your perceptions and your life as you read through *Restored and Forgiven, The Power of Restorative Justice.*

—**SHAWN VERHEY**, MANAGING CHAPLIN, HMP YOI THORN CROSS

THE JOURNEY OF FORGIVENESS

"Remember, you don't forgive someone for his or her sake—you forgive them for your sake."

"To forgive is to set a prisoner free and discover that the prisoner was you."

"Unforgiveness is like getting bitten by a poisonous snake."

"Forgiveness is not a sign of weakness; it is a sign of strength."

"When you hold resentment toward another, you are bound to that person or action by an emotional link that is stronger than steel. Forgiveness is the only way to dissolve that link and get free." — Katherine Ponder

"The best way to defeat your enemy is to forgive them."
—Nelson Mandela

There is a good saying: God doesn't call the qualified, He qualifies the called.

Since Christopher was taken from us, God has used us in a powerful way.

He has opened so many doors. It has been a privilege to work with so many inspiring people. He and they have encouraged us to carry on with what we are doing.

We could never have envisioned any of what you have read in this book, but our God is amazing.

He restored us with His precious gold. The cracks are still there but we are whole again and stronger than we ever were.

Forgiving Christopher's killers was the hardest, and at the same time the best, thing we could have ever done because it not only set them free, it set us free from the poison of unforgiveness.

Forgiveness is not how you feel or an emotion. It is a daily choice. You don't wake up one day and say, "I forgive"; it is an ongoing journey.

Forgiveness doesn't excuse people's behavior. It doesn't dismiss your feelings. We still feel angry at times, particularly at birthdays and other significant anniversaries.

The Bible says in 2 Corinthians 12:9:

> *"My grace is sufficient for you, for my power is made perfect in weakness." Therefore, I will boast all the more gladly about my weaknesses, so that Christ's power may rest on me.*

And that is why forgiveness is a choice, and we have chosen to take that path with God guiding us.

This was designed and drawn by a prison inmate
and donated to us.